SIKHISM
AT A GLANCE

The Sikhs and their Religion (Volume-1)

BHUPENDER SINGH

RIGI PUBLICATION

All right reserved

SIKHISM AT A GLANCE

The Sikhs and their Religion (Volume-1)

BY

BHUPENDER SINGH

Originally published in India

ISBN: 978-93-86447-52-4
Published by RIGI PUBLICATION

777, Street no.9, Krishna Nagar
Khanna-141401 (Punjab), India
Website: www.rigipublication.com
Email: info@rigipublication.com
Phone: +91-9357710014, +91-9465468291

PREFACE

The present day reader has no time for voluminous literature; he wants the essence of all salient features presented to him in a simple and concise form that he can easily comprehend. This is more so with the reader who is not well conversant or new to Sikh history and religion and wants to know what the religion is all about. Keeping their need in mind this small, compact book has been written for those lay readers who have neither the leisure nor the patience to go into details. The book gives a bird's-eye view with a humble endeavour to be objective and succinct. It is written more from a historical and pragmatic point of view rather than religious. The language used is simple and devoid of all technicalities, basically it is a statement of facts and figures.

The Sikhs are distinguished throughout the world as farmers and a great military people. The Khalsa has achieved a world-wide renown in the matter of bravery and there is great admiration and value for the Sikh soldier. Yet in spite of all the literature there is little known regarding their religion.

Unlike the days of yore when the Sikhs were unlettered because of over a century of persecution, the Sikhs today are erudite and there is a plethora of literature available. Sikh scriptures, annals and chronicles have been translated into English and other languages and a lot of study and research in various fields has been done. However, there are aspects that still require more study. I shall succeed in my aim and effort if the book proves to be handy and kindles interest in the reader.

*The book has been written with an open mind. Corrections, criticism and suggestions are welcome.

ACKNOWLEDGMENTS

I am indebted to Ms Rabinder Powar, professor of English in the Punjabi University Patiala for reading the manuscript and making corrections and valuable suggestions; to Mr. Parminder Kumar, Branch Manager and his Assistant Manager Mr. Ravi Shankar Mishra of Karnataka Bank Ltd. (Jodhpur) and also to Ms. Shruti Purohit and Mr. Punit Nepalia of the Equitas Small Finance Bank (Jodhpur) for their immense support and assistance in computer work.

CONTENTS

APPENDICES

THE LAND, CLIMATE, PEOPLE AND TIMES

The name: ***Punjab***

During the Vedic age, when the Aryans arrived in India, they found seven rivers and named the land Sapt Sindhva, the land of the seven seas. The Aryans were followed by the Persians and they called it the Hafta Haindva (this name is found in the *Zend-Avesta*, the holy book of the Parsees or Zoroastrians). Later in the Epic age, when the River Saraswati dried up (losing itself in the Thar Desert of Rajasthan), the River Indus was also excluded (since it marked only the extreme western boundary of the land) and the province was renamed after the remaining five rivers as Pentopotamia or the **Panj-ab**, the land of the five waters (rivers).

In the ancient period Punjab was also known as **Madra Desha** (after Madri, the mother of Pandavas), **Uttrarapath** or the northern country (this name appears in Buddhist literature), **Panchnad,** or Punjab (land of five rivers) and for several centuries as **Taki** or **Tak Desa**. Historically, Punjab as the name of the region finds mention in the writings of the 14th century AD, Arab marabout Ibn-Batuta[1].

 Punjab is the land of five rivers. The five rivers of Punjab are the **Jhelum** (Hydaspes), the **Chenab,** the **Ravi,** the **Beas,** and the **Sutlej**. Punjab is also a land of five doabs situated between these rivers. The mesopotamias or intra-fluvial tracts are known in the Punjab as **doabs** – two waters (land between two rivers). Barring the doabs between the Indus and the Jhelum and the Sutlej and the Jumna, they are known by a combination of the names of the two rivers between which they lie. The **Bist Doab** or the Bist-Jullundur Doab situated between the rivers Beas and Sutlej; the **Bari Doab** situated between the rivers Beas and the Ravi; the **Rechna Doab** situated between the rivers Ravi and Chenab; the **Chaj Doab** situated between the rivers Chenab and the Jhelum and the **Sindh Sagar Doab**, situated between the rivers Indus and Jhelum.

The territory between the Beas and the Ravi is known as **Majha**; between the Beas and the Sutlej **Doaba** and the area between the Sutlej and Ghaggar[2] is called **Malwa**. The homeland of the vast majority of the Sikhs is in the doabs between the Chenab and the Jumna. Since the river Sutlej runs through the middle of the zone of the main concentration of Sikh population, historians refer to the region west of the river as the **Trans-Sutlej** and that east of the river as the **Cis-Sutlej**. This division corresponds roughly to the traditional division of the Punjab into **Majha (Amritsar region)** and **Malwa (Sirhind region)**. The regions mentioned above are the predominant areas that witnessed most of the historical events related to the Sikhs.

The word Sikh is derived from the Sanskrit word *sishya*, meaning learner, disciple or pupil. The Punjabi form of the word was Sikh and came to be used for the disciples or followers of Guru Nanak (1469-1539) and his nine successors.

Punjab is a **land** of extremes. The country is either a long, monotonous stretch of land as flat as a pancake, or it suddenly turns into steep hills or rugged snow-capped mountains. The rivers and streams are either trickles, getting lost in the wide sandy wastes or they rage with floods spreading destruction far beyond the banks. The pulverized dust changes to slimy mud when a sudden torrential rain descends and halts all traffic except that of the sturdy ox or bullock-cart or the modern day tractor.

Today, nothing remains of the dense forests that once covered large tracts of Punjab. These forests were abound with a diversity of flora and fauna till the mid 19th century. They were home to a teeming variety of wild life that comprised lions, tigers, leopards, panthers, bears, wolves, hyenas, wild boars, *nilgai*, and many varieties of deer. Animals like rhinoceros (mentioned in Babar Nama) and perhaps elephants also roamed these jungles that existed in the north up to the 16th century. In Central Punjab there was the notorious *Lakhi* (the forest of a hundred thousand trees), which gave refuge to Sikh fugitives from their tormentors. There were equally dense forests in the Jullundur Doab and one long stretch of wood-land from Ludhiana to Karnal. The jungles survived the onslaught of foreign armies but succumbed to the avarice of man. The indiscriminate felling of trees and slaughter of game in the 19th and 20th century gave way to desolate wasteland. The desert with its camel and goats - the only animals which can thrive on cacti and shrub - are a phenomenon of recent times.

The climate, of Punjab too, has extremes as it ranges from excessive cold in winter to burning hot in summer. Extremes of temperature and two monsoons (summer and winter) produce a variety of seasons and a constantly changing landscape.

The spring is traditionally ushered in on *Basant panchami*, which falls early in the month of February. It is blossom time in Punjab and all plants are in flower. The country is a mass of green wheat fields with yellow flowers of mustard dotting the landscape. Peasants supplement the rain by canal water, or, where there are no canals, by Persian wheels (before the Persian wheels, there was the Charas[3]) turned by bullocks or camels and in present times there is the Tube well. The area around these wells abounds in a variety of vegetables. Then the wheat fields ripen and turn to golden brown and spring gives way to summer. The wheat is harvested and the country looks like a barren waste, with clouds of dust swirling about. The temperatures soar and the blazing inferno lasts from the end of April to the end of June. This is when the succulent mango season commences; there are grapes, melons and watermelons to boot.

In July the rains come. The monsoon makes a spectacular entry. There are flashes of lightning and thunder followed by the rain. The first few showers are welcome and a pleasant fragrance rises from the earth. It gladdens the spirits and there is rejoicing. Thereafter the monsoon bursts in all its fury and it rains cats and dogs for two months (July and August). The rain comes in torrents and with violence, day after day and continues for hours; things turn moist and soggy and the humidity gets on your nerves. The incessant downpours turn the land into a vast swamp and the country side green. By the time the monsoon is over, it is cool again. The dust settles and the area is green once more. October and November are the months for fairs and festivals.

Once again there is a change and it turns into winter time. It is bitingly cold with temperatures dropping below zero. The cold winds coming off the mountains to the north penetrate the heaviest clothing. The starlit nights are cold and frosty and the bright days with blue skies are full of sun shine. It is time to have *sarson da saag*, *makki de roti*, curd and butter washed down with *lassi* (butter milk). This is also the season for sugarcane and *kinu* juice. The sugarcane is cut, its juice squeezed out, boiled in large cauldrons and solidified into dark brown cakes (jaggery or *gurh*). *Kinu* is extensively cultivated and marketed. The *kinu* and *malta* are citrus fruits, a hybrid of orange and *mausami* (sweet lime). It is indeed salubrious climate with plenty to eat and drink.

It is small wonder that the Punjabi people, living outdoors close to the soil most of the time, are sensitive to nature in her rapidly changing moods. The distant forbears of the Sikhs, the Aryans, show this appreciation of nature in Vedic hymns and so do the Sikh Gurus (Guru Nanak's Bara Maha – The Twelve Months).

There are four main seasonal festivals of Punjab viz. *Lorhi*, the festival of bonfires (made of cow dung cakes and wood) celebrated on 13 January, with the distribution of sweets to mark the decline of winter; *Holi*, the festival of colours, celebrated in mid-March (the Sikhs celebrate it as *Hola Mohalla* with mock battles and martial arts); *Basakhi*, the spring harvest festival and the birth of the Khalsa, celebrated on 13 April and Deepawali, the festival of lights, celebrated in early November. *Basakhi* is celebrated with much fervour and gaiety, the males perform the *Bhangra* and the ladies the *Gidda* dance.

The people of such an area have to be hardy and adaptable in order to bear and survive such harsh, extremes of climate and onslaughts of foreign invasions. The Punjab, being the main gateway into India, was fated to be the unceasing battle field and the first home of all conquerors. Few invaders, brought women with them, and most of those who settled in their conquered domains picked up local females as wives and mistresses. Thus the coming of many conquering races made the society a multilingual and a multi-religious one. Out of this amalgam of blood were born the Punjabi people and from the bedlam of tongues the Punjabi language. It was but obvious that the multiplicity of faiths and the babel of varied prayers of their forefathers would give birth to a new faith for the people of the Punjab.

With the passage of time the different races that had come together in the Punjab had lost the nostalgic memories of the land of their origin and developed affection for the land of their adoption. They now had a common language – Punjabi. Although the Punjabis were acrimoniously divided into Muslims and Hindus, attempts had been made to reconcile the two faiths with a desire to live in harmony. There was a *Sufi* movement in Islam and *Bhakti* cult in Hinduism. It was left to Nanak and the Sikh Gurus to harness the spirit of tolerance and give it a positive shape.

The times, during this period were bad and turbulent. Punjab was being devastated by a series of invasions and struggle for power. Might was right and tyranny and persecutions were rampant. Trials (if any) were conducted quickly, and sentences speedily executed. The country had been ruled by foreign invaders for a long time. The rulers were whimsical and inhuman and the plight of the masses miserable. The common man was maltreated by the ruling class aided by local government functionaries. People were divided among themselves on the basis of caste and the high castes ill treated the low castes. The priestly class kept exploiting the ignorant masses. The condition of women was deplorable. The chaotic times and topsy-turvy conditions of the country are aptly depicted in Guru Nanak's verse:

> The age is like a knife
>
> Kings are butchers
>
> The law hath taken wing and flown;
>
> In the dark night of falsehood
>
> I cannot espy the rising of the moon of truth;
>
> I have searched everywhere and wearied of the quest;
>
> In the dusk I cannot find my path.
>
> Pride that is within is the root of sorrow
>
> Oh! Nanak how shall we be saved
>
> (On the morrow)?

Majh ki Var

[1]**Ibn Batuta** (1304-69), the noted writer and traveller, in his 27 years of wandering through Africa, Asia and Europe, covered 75,000 miles (1, 20,000 km.) thus out wandering the Venetian merchant and traveller Marco Polo (1254-1324). Marco Polo had journeyed from Europe to Asia (1271-95) travelling along the Silk Road and reached the court of Kublai Khan (1274). He spent about 17 years in China and the Mongol emperor sent him on several fact finding missions to distant lands.

[2]**The Ghaggar** is an intermittent or seasonal river, flowing during the monsoon rains. The river has its source in the Shivalik Hills of Himachal Pradesh and then runs southwest into Haryana, passing through Pinjore, Ambala and southwest of Sirsa. Thereafter it enters Rajasthan and going past Bikaner it disappears in the Thar Desert.

[3]**Charas** was a means of drawing water from a well, for irrigation. The oxen/camel moved forward pulling out water from the well in a large leather container. A human would then turn the container upside down, pouring the water into the irrigation drain, dug in the ground and the process would be repeated. The Charas in turn gave way to the Persian wheel, which was a later day innovation and today there is the electric driven tube-well.

- Although Punjab is one region, it is at present divided into three, each area being the home of a distinct religious community. In August 1947 the province was partitioned into two. The larger part, the West Punjab, then richer in agricultural assets and potential and mineral wealth became **Pakistan** with a Muslim majority. Subsequently, in November 1966, the Indian Punjab was divided into two states **Punjab** and **Haryana**. These divisions do not pay due heed to cultural similarities, the shared past of the three communities – Muslim, Sikh and Hindu nor of the uniqueness of the area as such from the rest of the sub-continent.

THE TEN SIKH GURUS

GURU NANAK

(15 APRIL 1469 - 22 SEPTEMBER 1539)

Guru Nanak Dev was the son of Hindu parents, Mehta Kalyan Das **Bedi** (Mehta Kalu) and Mata Tripta. Unlike Mahavira and Buddha, Nanak was not born to affluent parents. His father was a petty official (village patwari). He was born on 15 April 1469 in Talwandi (Nankana Sahib), Pakistan. But his birthday is celebrated on full moon (Puranmashi) in the month of Kattak (generally November), because it was on this day in 1499 that he came out of the Rivulet Vein after three days and nights and after having attained Divine revelation (Brahm Gyan). He was named Nanak because like his elder sister Nanki (about 05 years older than him), he was born in the home of his mother, Tripta and like her named after his maternal home, Nankey. Guru Nanak was married to Bibi Sulakhni the daughter of Mool Chand Chona of Batala and had two sons Sri Chand (an ascetic, who found the Udasi Sect) and Lakhmi Das. His sister Nanki's husband was Jai Ram (Guru Nanak's brother-in- law).

Guru Nanak was a great reformer and denounced asceticism, renunciation, austerity, penances, mortification, celibacy, priest craft, idolatry, ritual, superstition, dogma, caste system, religious intolerance and prejudice against women. Guru Nanak's first message after he was ordained was "There is no Hindu; There is no Mussalman." All are human beings. He worked and preached for a casteless and egalitarian society. He took practical steps to break the vicious hold of caste by starting a free community kitchen – *Guru Ka Langar* and persuaded his followers, irrespective of their caste, to eat together. He had to combat the furious bigotry of the Muslim and the deep-rooted superstition of the Hindu. Guru Nanak substituted love in place of all the intricate doctrines of faith. And the practical expression of this love was service (sewa). One can see no higher record of service in the annals of mankind than that of the Sikhs. The emancipation and empowerment of women and gender equality had an important place in his teachings. He himself summed up his message in three commandments: *Kirt karo, nam japo, vand chako –* work, worship and give in charity.

Guru Nanak made four long journeys (Udasis). He went as far as Assam in the east, Ceylon (Sri Lanka) in the south, Nepal and Tibet in the north, and Mecca and Baghdad in the west. Thus for forty long years, he travelled throughout the length and breadth of India to study the various religions in practice. Wherever he went, he is remembered and revered even today. Guru Nanak's preaching methods were unconventional and dramatic. It is said that on a trip to Brindaban he donned the saffron jacket of a sadhu, the woolen shirt of a faqir and the hat of a Qalandar dervish. His hallmark was utter **simplicity** so that what he said could be understood by the rustic as well as by the sophisticated and he used Punjabi vernacular instead of Sanskrit for his religious poems. His constant companions and disciples were Mardana, a Muslim rabab-player, and Bala, a Hindu. Guru Nanak identified himself with the lowest of the low. He refers to himself as "Nanak, the servant," "Nanak the low-caste" and "Nanak, the humble." Says Guru Nanak:

> Among the low, let my caste be the lowest.
> Of the lowly, let me the lowliest be.
> O Nanak, let such be the men I know,
> With such men let me keep company.
> Why must I try to emulate the great?

As a boy, while grazing cattle, he fell asleep under a shady tree and soon when the sun shone on his face, it is said a **cobra**, provided him shade with its hood. One day Nanak's father gave him some money and asked him to go and invest it in *'Sacha Sauda'* (good bargain/ business). On his way he met a group of starving *sadhus*. So he used the money to buy provisions for them and returned home empty handed. While facing the wrath of his father, he said, "What better bargain can there be than feeding the poor and hungry."

At **Hardwar**, while bathing in the sacred Ganges; he saw people offering water to the sun, so he began to throw handfuls of water towards the West. When questioned, he replied that if the water could reach their ancestors in heaven so far away, it would certainly reach his parched fields in Punjab.

On visiting **Mecca**, the weary Nanak went to sleep with his feet towards Kaaba. When there was an outcry on the sacrilege, he had committed, he told them to turn his feet in the direction where God did not reside.

On reaching Saidpur (today's Eminabad in Pakistan) Baba Nanak found that Malik Bhago, a man who had amassed untold wealth, was holding a sacrificial feast to which all holy men including Guru Nanak were invited. The Guru preferred to remain away and stay with **Bhai Lalo**, a poor carpenter. He answered Malik Bhago's fury by saying that there was blood in his food, but milk and honey in Bhai Lalo's bread, because it had been earned by him with hard toil and sweat. As for worldly wealth he maintained that it cannot be collected without unfair means and when you die, it doesn't go with you.

At **Jagannath Puri**, Guru Nanak found that the priests attached more importance to rituals. Throughout the day they made elaborate arrangements with perfumed trays of flowers and burning candles in order to propitiate the deity. They called it *arti* (adoration of God by a ceremony of lights). Guru Nanak sat outside the temple and started singing with Mardana playing on the *rabab*:

> The sky is the tray,
> The sun and moon are the lights
> And the stars the jewels.
> Sandalwood fragrance is the incense,
> The wind is the fly – whisk
> And all the forests your flowers.
> What a wonderful *arti* it is!

There are many more stories like this about Guru Nanak and his ways of teaching. His teachings are unique and ever fresh and they fired the imagination of the people of Punjab. He never made any claims to kinship with God nor invests his hymns with the garb of sanctity. He was content to be a teacher (guru). He was a great prophet, seer, sage and poet. Nanak is still remembered in Punjab as the King of holy men, the Guru of the Hindus, and *Pir* of the Mussalmans:

Baba Nanak shah *fakir*
Hindu ka guru, mussalman ka *pir*

There is only one teacher of teachers, who appears in many forms.
In whatever house (of faith) the Creator's praises are sung,
Follow that house, in that house rests true greatness.
Guru Nanak - SGGS-12.

GURU ANGAD

(31 MARCH 1504 – 29 MARCH 1552)

Lehna, a Khatri of the **Trihan** sub-caste, had been a devout Hindu and devotee of goddess Durga before he met Nanak. At the very first meeting he fell under the spell of the Guru's words and abandoned everything including his business, in order to devote himself whole heartedly to the service of Nanak and his Sikhs. Twice Guru Nanak persuaded him to return to his family, but both times he came back. The sincere, selfless devotion and dedication of Lehna, now called Angad, (Guru Nanak said, "thou art Angad, a part of my body.") convinced the Guru that he would make a better leader than his sons. An additional factor was that Angad had a sizeable following of his own, which was following their leader into the Sikh fold. Angad became Guru on **14 June 1539**. Guru Angad was a great lover of children and very keen on physical fitness. In Sikh history, there is a strong tradition that when Humayun was on the run after his defeat in the battle of Kanauj, he waited on Guru Angad at Khadur. Since Humyaun had to wait, he tried to unsheathe his sword. The Guru reminded him of his cowardice against Sher Shah Suri, where he should have wielded the sword. He felt ashamed and sought the Guru's blessings for the recovery of his lost throne. The guru blessed him and advised him to leave the country in his own interest.

Guru Angad did a lot to popularize Sikhism. His main contributions were:

- He popularized the *Gurumukhi* script.

- He strengthened and devotedly encouraged the institution of Langar.

- He collected Guru Nanak's *Bani* (sayings and hymns) and got his *Janam Sakhi* (biography) by Bhai Bala written by Pairha Mokha in Gurumukhi script.

- By his tact and humility, he was able to prevent the schism between his Sikhs and the followers of Guru Nanak's son, Sri Chand (*Udasis –* those who renounce the world).

GURU AMAR DAS

(5 MAY 1479 – 01 SEPTEMBER 1574)

Angad had two sons but he chose a seventy-three year old humble and dedicated disciple, Amar Das, a Khatri of the **Bhalla** sub-caste to succeed him as the **third** Guru on **29 March 1552**. Guru Amar Das had been a zealous Vaishnavite and a devout Hindu enjoying a reputation for kindness and piety long before his coming into the Sikh fold. He made the langar an integral institution of the Sikh church by insisting that anyone who wanted to see him had to accept his hospitality by eating with his disciples. The Guru's visitors increased manifold. Among the people who visited was Emperor Akbar. The Emperor granted the revenue of several villages to the Guru's daughter, Bibi Bhani, as a marriage gift. It is at this place that **Amritsar** came to be established in due course.

Guru Amar Das had more copies made of the hymns of Nanak and Angad and added to them his own compositions and those of other *Bhaktas* whose teachings were in conformity with those of Nanak. Since the anthology was in Punjabi, it gained enormous popularity among the masses, who did not understand either Sanskrit or Arabic. It reduced the importance of the Brahmin priests, who maintained a strict monopoly over the knowledge of the sacred texts, and that of the mullahs, who alone could interpret the Koran. He passed away at a ripe old age of ninety-five.

The main contributions of Guru Amar Das to the Sikh faith were:

- Due to scarcity of water, he got a '*Baoli*' (deep well) dug at Goindwal.

- Since he alone could not cater to the needs of thousands of   devotees, he increased the number of *manjis* or *parchar kendras* (parishes) to 22 and appointed accomplished agents (*masands*), to organize, worship and collect offerings.

- He introduced social reforms and condemned the practice of Sati and *purdah* (veil) among women. He advocated monogamy and encouraged widow remarriage.

- He simplified death and birth ceremonies.

- In order to remove the shackles of caste and the gulf and barriers between the rich and poor everyone had to dine in the Langar before they could see the Guru.

- The festivals of Diwali, Holi and Baisakhi were celebrated in a new way.

GURU RAM DAS

(25 SEPTEMBER 1534 – 02 SEPTEMBER 1581)

Guru Amar Das did not consider any of his two sons fit enough and chose instead his son-in-law, Ram Das, a Khatri of the **Sodhi** sub-caste who had been living with him for some years to succeed him as the **fourth** Guru on **01 September 1574**. In his earlier days Ram Das was known as Bhai Jetha. According to Sikh chronicles, Jetha was orphaned at the age of seven (he lost his mother when he was two and father at the age of seven) and was brought up by his maternal grandmother. Ram Das was a man of great humility and had spent the better part of his life in administration of the parishes (religious areas) and the service of the community. Because of his commitment, selfless service and sterling qualities of head and heart, Guru Amar Das was so pleased with him that he gave his daughter Bibi Bhani in marriage to him (around 1553). Later after having appointed him as his successor, he made the *Guru-gaddi* hereditary in his family.

His inputs towards the Sikh Religion were:

- He had a tank dug at the site granted to his wife by Emperor Akbar on the advice of his father-in-law (Guru Amar Das). When he became Guru, he moved to the neighbourhood of the tank and started building a town around it. The town came to be known after him as *Guru Ka chack, Chack Ram Das*, or *Ram Das Pura*. Today it is **Amritsar**.

- Since Guru Ram Das needed funds, he invited fifty-two types of artisans and tradesmen to set up business in the town. He also asked the *Masands* (agents) to collect donations from his followers.

- In order to popularize the religion, he sent missionaries to distant parts of the country. The most distinguished of these was Bhai Gurdas (the nephew of Guru Amar Das and compiler of *Adi* Granth under the direction of Guru Arjun), who spent some years preaching in Agra.

- Guru Ram Das had represented Guru Amar Das in the court of Emperor Akbar at Lahore in 1566-1567. This was in order to refute the allegations of the opponents of the Guru, who desired to proscribe the Sikh scriptures with the help of the Mughal state. The antagonists had to eat humble pie.

GURU ARJUN DEV

(15 APRIL 1563 – 30 MAY 1606)

Guru Arjun was the youngest of Guru Ram Das's three sons and was nominated as the **fifth** guru on **02 September 1581**. He was the first Guru to have been born a Sikh. In five years of travelling in Central

Punjab, Arjun brought into his fold thousands of Jats of the Majha tract, the sturdiest peasants of the Punjab. It is during this period that the Jat influx into Sikhism started. These brave people were to play a very prominent role in Sikh history and battles, in times to come.

The death of Akbar brought a sudden reversal in the policy of the Mughal state towards the Sikhs. In April-May, 1606 Prince Khusrav, the eldest son of Jehangir through his cousin Manbai (daughter of Raja Bhagwan Das of Amber) revolted against him. Guru Arjun Dev bestowed his benediction on Khusrav when the latter visited him on his way from Agra to Lahore. The Guru kept an open house and would bless anyone who came to him. The new Emperor Jehangir could not stand the growing popularity and power of the Guru and as an excuse held him guilty of supporting a rebel. To add fuel to fire were the Guru's elder brother Prithi Chand (overlooked to be Guru) and Chandu Shah (a Hindu banker whose daughter's hand Arjun had refused to accept for his son). A heavy fine was levied on the Guru and, on his refusal to admit the charge of treason or pay the fine; he was arrested and tortured to death on 30 May 1606. This was a turning point in the history of Punjab.

The achievements of Guru Arjun were:

- He completed the tank at Amritsar and built the Golden Temple (Darbar Sahib or Harmandir Sahib) in it.

- He laid the foundation of Tarn Taran (1590), Kartarpur (1594) and Sri Hargobindpur (named after his son in 1595) on the banks of River Beas.

- He organized the *Masand* System on new lines. The devotees were asked to donate one tenth (tithe/*dushanj*) of their income.

- In order to improve the economic condition of the Sikhs, he encouraged them to trade (especially in horses).

- Trade thrived and the Guru's importance, wealth and power grew. He began to be addressed as the *Sacha Padshah* (the true Emperor).

- His monumental work was the compilation of the *Adi* Granth in August 1604. The Guru Granth Sahib was formally installed in the Golden Temple and Bhai Buddha was appointed the first reader or *granthi*.

GURU HARGOBIND

(14 JUNE 1595 – 03 MARCH 1644)

At the age of eleven, Guru Hargobind became the **sixth** Guru on **25 May 1606.** The furious Sikhs were ready to avenge the murder of their Guru Arjun. The young Guru Hargobind sat on the *Gurgaddi* fully armed with two swords girded around his waist, carrying the emblem of royalty on his turban and was addressed as Sacha Badshah. One sword symbolized spiritual power and the other temporal (**Miri and Piri**). Henceforth it was a **call to arms**. The Sikhs were asked to bring offerings of arms and horses instead of money. The first five Gurus were religious and social reformers; the last five had to take steps to carry on this work against increasingly hostile military forces.

On the complaints of Chandu (the banker), Meharban (son of Prithi Chand, Guru Arjun's elder brother) and other anti-Guru elements and also because of the pending fine imposed on the Guru's father (Arjun), Guru Hargobind was arrested and imprisoned in Gwalior fort. He spent a year or more in imprisonment. On release he was more cautious and resumed his martial activity. With the death of Jehangir and accession of the orthodox and religious fanatic Shah Jahan in 1627 A. D., the Guru had to fight four battles (in fact skirmishes), that were imposed on him. The four battles were: (a) Against Mukhlis Khan at Amritsar in May 1629. (b) Against Abdullah Khan at Sri Hargobindpur (Sep.1629). (c) Against Lalla Begh at Mehraj (near Nathana) in Nov.1631. (d) Against Kale Khan and Painde Khan at Kartarpur (Jalandhar) in 1634. It is remarkable that all these battles were won by the Guru and all the four enemy commanders were slain by him in duels.

The achievements of Guru Hargobind were:

- He had a standing army of eight hundred horses, three hundred horsemen, and sixty foot with fire arms and seven guns.

- He built a small fortress, Lohgarh (castle of steel) at Amritsar.

- Across the Harimandir, he built the **Akal Takht** (the throne of the Timeless God), where ballads extolling feats of heroism were heard instead of chants of hymns of peace and military plans discussed instead of religious discourses.

- In 1634 he founded the town of Kiratpur, a haven for refuge in the Shivalik foothills above Ropar.

The last days of his life were marred by domestic tragedies. Five members of his family, including three sons died one after the other and his grandson Dhirmal turned against him.

GURU HAR RAI

(16 JAN. 1630 – 07 OCT. 1661)

Guru Har Rai was the son of Baba Gurditta who had died in 1638 and grandson of Guru Hargobind. He became the **seventh** Guru on **08 March 1644**. Fitness rather than primogeniture was time and again the deciding factor. In less than a year after becoming Guru he was compelled to leave Kiratpur and retire further into the mountains. The Raja of Bilaspur, in whose territory Kiratpur was situated, was having trouble with the Mughal government and Har Rai feared that he and his men may get caught in this embroilment. He spent the next thirteen years in comparative seclusion in a small village (perhaps Taksal) in Sirmoor State. Later he tried to make up for this by conducting visits to various centers. During his time some notable landed families came into the Sikh fold. These included the princely families of Patiala, Nabha and Jind and also the families of Kaithal and Bagarian, whose descendants played a distinguished role in building the Sikh empire.

In the end of 1658, the Guru returned to Kiratpur. He befriended Dara Shikoh, the eldest son of Emperor Shah Jahan, who was a liberal and of Sufi persuasion, when the later visited him. This was sufficient to arouse the wrath of bigoted Aurangzeb, who after the war of succession, summoned Guru Har Rai to Delhi. The Guru sent his elder son Ram Rai to represent him. On being asked to explain a verse from the Guru Granth, Ram Rai succeeded in winning the confidence of Aurangzeb by manipulating a word. The Guru was displeased with this tampering and excommunicated him. Emperor Arungzeb, however, encouraged this rift between father and son and gave Ram Rai a *jagir* of land on which he built a gurudwara and **Dehra Dun** grew up around it. Till date it is the headquarters of the **Ram-Raiye sect**.

Guru Har Rai's seventeen years of Guruship was not marked by any spectacular events. Besides keeping a fighting force (no battle was ever forced on him) and some preaching missions, his tenure was not especially significant. Although he inherited a martial tradition and kept an army of 2,200 horsemen, as advised by his grandfather, he was a man of peace and hated bloodshed. "You can repair or rebuild a temple or a mosque, but not a broken heart," he said.

GURU HAR KRISHAN

(07 JULY 1656 – 30 MARCH 1664)

The investiture of Guru Har Krishan on **07 October, 1661** at the **age of five** did not suit Aurangzeb, who wanted to meddle in Sikh affairs. He summoned the infant Guru to Delhi with the intention of deciding the matter of Guruship between him and his elder brother Ram Rai. It is not very likely that Ram Rai, who was little more than a boy himself, could have pursued the matter of succession on his own initiative. Backing him were some crafty and malicious *masands,* who like the Emperor, wished to have the Guru as a puppet in their hands. Guru Har Krishan arrived in Delhi and stayed in the Bungalow (now turned into **Gurdwara Bangla Sahib**) of Mirza Raja Jai Singh of Amber (Jaipur). Aurangzeb was in no hurry to announce his arbitration (nor indeed would the Sikhs have paid any heed to it).

In those days Delhi was in the grip of a small-pox epidemic and Guru Har Krishan succumbed to it and was cremated at a site, where **Gurdwara Bala Sahib** stands today. At this time he was a little less than eight years old and had been Guru for two and a half years. On being asked about his successor, the Guru's last words were, "Baba Bakale."

GURU TEGH BAHADUR

(01 APRIL 1621 - 11 NOVEMBER 1675)

The saintly Guru Tegh Bahadur was the son of Guru Hargobind and the grand-uncle of Guru Har Krishan. He had retired to Baba Bakala, where he lived in seclusion and spent most of his time in prayer and meditation in a basement. A whole lot of Sodhi imposters (22 in number) had sprung up and all were claiming the *gaddi* (seat of guruship) after the demise of the eighth Guru. He was formally proclaimed as the **ninth Guru** on **11 August 1664** when he was **forty-four (44)** years old. Even then a few months passed in confusion. Eventually on the Diwali day (09 October 1664) he was located and identified by **Makhan Shah Lubana** and all doubts were put to rest.

The Guru was a man of retiring habits who did not wish to fight for his rights. As a result he was hounded wherever he went. At Amritsar the doors of the Harimandir were slammed in his face. But his very reluctance to press for recognition turned the masses in his favour. He founded the city of Anandpur (the haven of bliss) in the foothills of the Himalayas. Here he expected to find peace and solitude. But even here his kinsmen did not leave him alone. Ultimately he decided to leave Punjab until things became more congenial. He travelled through Delhi, U.P. and Bihar and arrived at Patna. Here, he left his family and moved on to Bengal and from there to Assam. He spent nearly three years in Assam before returning to his family and son (born in his absence) at Patna. But he could not spend much time with his family and infant son because there were urgent messages beckoning him to Punjab. On his arrival he found the population of

Sikhs and Hindus in a state of panic. The Emperor Aurangzeb had embarked on a policy of religious persecution, followed more vigorously than before. The guru's rivals had discreetly disappeared from the scene. Now it was left to him to instill confidence in the people. He exhorted them to stand firm and not to budge under duress. This was not palatable to the government at Delhi.

On 25 May 1675, a deputation of sixteen Kashmiri Brahmins, headed by **Kirpa Ram** reached Anandpur. They waited on the Guru and told him that Aurangzeb was converting the Kashmiris to Islam. After hearing their heart-rending complaints, Guru Tegh Bahadur pondered over the grave dilemma and asked the leader of the deputation to tell the administration that Guru Tegh Bahadur was their leader and if he embraces Islam, they would all follow suit. This suited the administration and the Guru was summoned to Delhi. At Delhi, in order to frighten the Guru, his three companions were tortured to death. Bhai **Mati Das** was sawn alive into two, Bhai **Dayal Das** was boiled alive in boiling water and **Sati Das** was roasted alive wrapped in cotton wool. On the Guru's refusal to accept Islam, he was asked to exhibit some of the miraculous powers that he was reputed to possess. Thereupon the Guru wrote something on a piece of paper and tied it with a string round his neck. This he said would prevent the executioner (Jalal-ud-Din of Samana) from cutting off his head. When the Guru's head was severed, the piece of paper was opened. It read: *Sis diya par sir na diya* – "I gave my head but not my secret." The **Gurdwara Sis Ganj** at Chandni Chowk (Delhi) marks the place where Guru Tegh Bahadur was martyred on 11 November 1675.

Guru Gobind Singh wrote of his father's martyrdom in the following words:

> To protect their right to wear their
> caste-marks and sacred threads,

> Did he in the dark age,
> perform the supreme sacrifice.

GURU GOBIND SINGH

(22 DECEMBER 1666 – 07 October 1708)

Guru Gobind Rai was only nine years old when he became the Guru on **11 November 1675.** In the sudden storm that followed Guru Tegh Bahadur's beheading, **Bhai Lakhi Shah Vanjara** lifted the dead body in one of his bullock carts and brought it to his hut in village Raisina. Here a pyre was prepared and the hut set on fire. **Gurdwara Rikab Ganj** (near Rashtrapati Bhawan, New Delhi) stands on this site today. The head was lifted by a devout Sikh, **Bhai Jaita (Jiwan Singh Rangreta)** and carried to Anandpur Sahib. The shock to the child Guru's mind and to other members of the family was tremendous. The place where the head was cremated in Anandpur is also called **Sis Ganj**.

For reasons of safety and security the leaders of the community moved Guru Gobind and his retinue further into the seclusion of the mountains, from Anandpur to Paonta. Guru Gobind fought about fourteen battles. Some of the battles were fought against the Rajput hill chiefs, some against the Mughals, and others against the combined forces of the Mughals and hill chiefs and yet others where the hill chiefs sided with the Guru against the Mughals. The reasons for the opposition of the hill Rajas to the Guru were their dislike of the growing power of the Guru in their region, the fear of the increasing insubordination of the lower castes, who had begun to turn to the casteless Sikh fraternity for leadership, the danger and fear of reprisal by the Mughal power at Delhi and lastly their opportunism. Thus it was a more or less love-hate relationship between them.

Guru Gobind's first baptism in steel was the battle of Bhangani (1686), against the combined forces of the hill chiefs and Pathans (mercenaries in the Sikh army who were won over by the hill rajas). Despite the desertions and numerical superiority of the enemy, the Sikhs (most of whom were Hindus of the trading castes) carried the day. The victory at Bhangani gave confidence to the young Guru to return to Anandpur. The Guru's second battle was fought at Nadaun (1687). This time it was the hill rajas who had requested the Guru to lead them against the Mughals. The initial round was won by the confederates. In spite of the victory the hill chiefs decided to come to terms with the Mughal commander in order to avoid the likelihood of another force being sent against them. Guru Gobind kept aloof and refused to enter into these discussions. The Mughal Emperor did not approve of this settlement because it was the defiance of his authority. He sent another force under Muazzam (later Bahadur Shah) and General Mirza Beg and they quickly reduced the hill chiefs to subservience. Mirza Beg had secret instructions not to bother the Guru (as per Sikh chronicles this was brought about by the good offices of one Nand Lal Goya, a Sikh poet of Persian, who had influence over the prince). The prince was looking into the future (Guru Gobind came to his support in the battle of succession) and Guru Gobind was left unmolested for twelve years.

Guru Gobind made optimum use of these twelve years of peace. He fortified the centre at Anandpur. He bought the neighbouring land and built the fortresses of Anandgarh, Keshgarh, Lohgarh and Fatehgarh. These years were also full of intellectual activity. The Guru was a polyglot. He knew Sanskrit and Persian in addition to Hindi and Punjabi and had knowledge of the Quran. He was a poet of considerable talent and composed poetry. Poets sought Guru Gobind's patronage and at one time there were fifty-two (52) poets in his court.

The prominent ones were Saina Pat, Bhai Nand Lal "Goya" and Bhai Mani Singh. The Guru pondered profoundly over the disunity and decadence that had crept into the movement launched by Guru Nanak. He found that the two main causes which had contributed to the state of affairs were the squabbles over the succession to the guruship and the corruption of the *masands*. With one stroke of his pen, he did away with the *masands* by pronouncing an excommunication on the whole lot of them. Later he was to do away with a living Guru also.

The Guru sent *hukamnamas* to his Sikhs to gather at Anandpur Sahib for the Vaisakh festival. On the first of Vaisakh **29 March 1699, he created the Khalsa** and gave them the five Ks (discussed in the next chapter). The emergence of a large and aggressive group (who when aroused were a force of bellicose, intrepid warriors with an innate love of war), in their midst made the hill rajas nervous and they feared the wrath of the Mughal government. The hill men encircled Anandpur and stopped all supplies of food-grains. The Guru had to move out to a small village **Nirmoh**. The Emperor's forces joined the hill men and they invested Nirmoh. The Khalsa held them at bay and, after twenty-four hours of continuous fighting, broke through the besiegers and found refuge at **Basali**. The Raja of Bilaspur made one more attempt to annihilate the Guru's forces, but badly beaten, made terms with the Guru, and the Khalsa returned to Anandpur.

Here preparations were made for more serious trouble that lay ahead. The anticipated trouble did not take long in coming. Anandpur was once again besieged by a combined force of the hill men and Mughals. Again the stock of food in Anandpur ran out and attempts to break out were frustrated. The Sikhs held on doggedly until the besiegers were as wearied of fighting as they themselves were. The enemy knew that the Sikhs would not surrender and fight to the last man. Guru Gobind was offered promises of safe conduct if he evacuated Anandpur. The Guru did not believe these promises and oaths, but the Sikhs were breaking down under pressure. Forty Sikhs from Majha disowned the Guru and after giving this in writing deserted the field. Ultimately under immense compulsion the Guru ordered the evacuation of the fort. He moved out with his family and a small band of soldiers who remained with him.

True to his suspicion, he had not gone far, when contrary to their solemn oaths, the imperial forces and hill men came in pursuit. Skirmishes commenced from Kiratpur onwards. At Shahi Tibbi a small band of fifty Sikhs under **Udai Singh** fell back and held the enemy until they were all killed. Again, close to the banks of Sarsa river, when it was almost dawn **Jiwan Singh** with a hundred men fought another delaying action to harass the pursuers and gain time. Guru Gobind entrusted his mother, wife and two younger sons to **Gangu** a Brahmin servant and moved southwards. While crossing River Sarsa, which was in spate many Sikh soldiers were swept away and many drowned in the river. There was great loss to valuable literature and property. The rearguard actions gave the Guru time to reach Chamkaur, where he and forty men who were left with him built a stockade and decided to fight to a finish.

The chivalrous little band kept the enemy at bay. Every few hours some of them would emerge, rush out and fight to the end. Ultimately only five of the forty remained. Among those who fell at **Chamkaur**, were the Guru's elder sons, **Ajit Singh** and **Jujhar Singh**. When all seemed lost, a Sikh who resembled the Guru put on his dress and went out to fight. While the enemy was celebrating their kill, the Guru made good his escape. At Machiwara two Pathans, **Nabi Khan** and **Ghani Khan**, whom the Guru had known earlier, saved his life. They put the Guru in a curtained palanquin and passed the Mughal sentries with the explanation that they were carrying their *pir* (*Uch da Pir*).

That was the end of the pursuit as far as the Guru was concerned. He arrived at the village of Jatpura. It is here that he wrote the famous *Zafarnama* (the epistle of victory) and learnt of the execution of his two remaining younger sons, **Zorawar Singh**, aged nine, and **Fateh Singh**, aged seven, and the death of his mother because of the shock. The children had been betrayed by the Brahmin cook Gangu and bricked alive on the orders of **Wazir Khan, the governor of Sirhind** on the advice and instigation of one **Sucha Nand**, his adviser. The Sikhs hold both of them equally responsible for the murders.

The news of the dastardly murders spread all over the countryside and thousands of Sikhs flocked to the Guru's camp at Kot Kapura. Among the people marching to meet the Guru were the **forty deserters** of Anandpur, who had been chided, taunted and humiliated by their womenfolk. Egging them on was a lady, **Mai Bhago.** Guru Gobind Singh prepared to meet Wazir Khan's forces near a pond in village Khidrana, now **Muktsar** (the pool of salvation). The forty deserters reached on time to receive the enemy in the bushes, below a mound. For them it was a matter of do or die for they had to retrieve their lost prestige. They took the enemy head on and fought tooth and nail to the last. In the end, after taking a heavy toll of the enemy forces, the gallant forty, either fell dead or lay mortally wounded. The Guru now had a sizable force to scatter the enemy. After the **Battle of Muktsar** (29 December 1705), **Bhai Mahan Singh**, the leader of the forty, died in the Guru's lap. His last wish was that the Guru should tear up the disclaimer and the Guru willing obliged. The lady Mai Bhago also lay wounded, but she survived. These forty are known as the *Chali muktas* (the emancipated ones).

The Guru spent almost a year in the country around Muktsar. Hundreds of thousands of Jats of the Malwa region accepted baptism and joined the Khalsa fraternity; among them were the ancestors of the house of **Patiala**, **Nabha**, and **Jind** whose families had already become Sikhs. Gobind retired for some time to the village of Talwandi Sabo (now called dam dama, "breathing place"). Here along with Bhai Mani Singh, he gave final shape to the Guru Granth by incorporating the writings of his father in it. In addition, he collected his own writings and put them in a separate Granth called *Dasam Granth*. From here he also sent a letter (not Zafarnama) to Aurangzeb. Apparently moved by the letter Aurangzeb issued orders that the Guru was not to be molested any further and invited the Guru to meet him.

In the war of succession after the death of Aurangzeb (02 March 1707), Guru Gobind, in order to repay the old debt sent a detachment of Sikh horsemen to help Bahadur Shah. The detachment fought in the **battle of Jajau on June 8, 1707**. When Bahadur Shah was firmly installed in the royal throne, Guru Gobind Singh paid him a formal visit and spent four months with him in Agra. Subsequently he accompanied him to the Deccan. At Nanded he met **Banda Singh Bahadur** (the famous Sikh general). Later at Nanded, two young Pathans **Gul Khan**, alias **Jamshed Khan** and his brother **Ata Ullah** entered his tent and, finding the Guru alone stabbed him. Since the assassins were slain immediately, the motive of the attack was never known. The Guru passed away an hour and a half after midnight on October 7, 1708. He bestowed the Guruship on the Guru Granth Sahib. Here was a man who sacrificed all that he had for the cause that he espoused – his parents, four sons, a large number of followers and ultimately himself.

FAMILY TREE OF SODHI CLAN
(Guru Ram Das To Guru Gobind Singh)

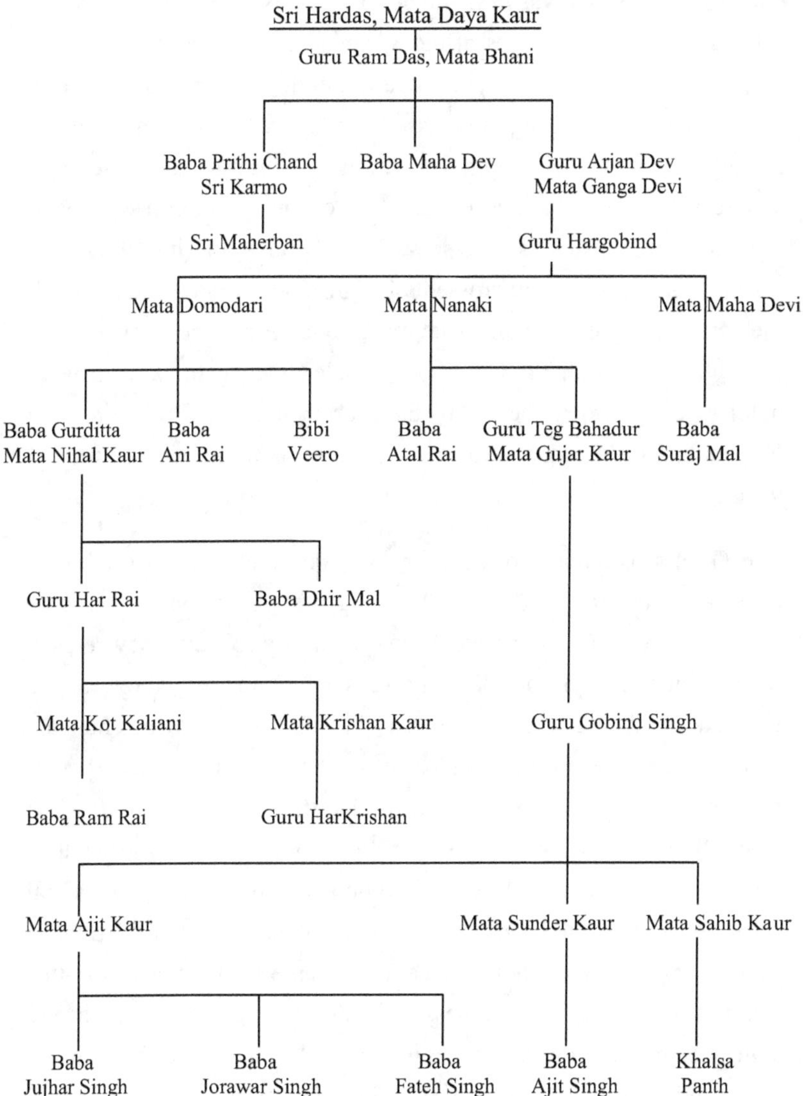

THE KHALSA AND THE FIVE Ks
FROM THE TRANQUIL SIKH TO THE BELLICOSE KHALSA

Guru Gobind Singh was determined to seek justice for the murder of his father and the atrocities of the Mughals and also save the honour of his country. On assessing the situation in the country, he found that a foreign race was ruling the masses and had reduced them to virtual slavery. They were holding the nation to ransom and oppression, suppression, repression and exploitation of the common people were rampant in the state. The worst was that tyranny and humiliation of the repressed masses had crossed all limits and the state had assumed the form of a purely Islamic nation. There were forced conversions and religious apartheid. The minority ruled the majority, who were helpless and at their mercy. In the words of Dr S. R. Sharma the Hindus had been reduced to mere "hewers of wood and drawers of water."

The Guru's paramount observation was that the people were meek, timid and cowardly and divided among themselves on the basis of caste and creed. On being confronted or in a dire state, they refused their identity and begged their oppressors for mercy. Above all he realised that being truthful, good, right, just, peace loving, humane and principled had no value unless it was backed with power. History had proved this time and time again. The famous quote of Mao Tse Tung "Power grows out of the barrel of a gun," amply justifies this. Guru Gobind had a keen insight into human nature and was a natural leader of men. He felt sad on seeing the pathetic plight of the people; he contemplated the whole problem and came to the conclusion that nothing could be achieved unless assiduous preparations were made to fight tyranny. He defined his mission as: "to uphold right in every place and destroy sin and evil; that right may triumph, the good may live and tyranny is uprooted from the country." He said, "When all modes of redressing a wrong have failed; raising the sword is just and pious." and "Take the broom of divine knowledge in thy hand and sweep away the filth of timidity." Thus did he embark on his mission of making the sparrow hunt the hawk; converting the jackal into a lion and making one man fight a legion.

On Vaisakhi day (**29 March 1699**) Guru Gobind Singh put his plan into action. He invited the Sikhs to assemble en masse at Anandpur Sahib for the Vaisakhi festival. He addressed the gathering and selected five Sikhs. They were **Daya Ram** a Khatri from Lahore, **Dharam Das** a Jat from Hastinapur (Meerut-U.P.), **Himmat Rai** a water carrier from Jagan-nath Puri (Orissa), **Mukahm Chand** a cheemba (calico printer) from Dwarka (Gujrat) and **Sahib Chand** a barber from Bidar. They were all in their thirties and are known as the Punj Payare (Five Beloved Ones). The Guru baptized the five (who came from different Hindu castes) by making them drink *Amrit* (nectar of immortality), prepared by a *khanda* (double edged sword) from the same bowl. They were thus initiated into the casteless fighting fraternity which he named the **Khalsa** (the chosen ones). Thus did Guru Gobind Singh transform his followers from the pacifist Sikh into the militant Khalsa.

The initiated ones were enjoined to suffix Singh (lion) to their names, which meant that all baptized Sikhs belonged to one family. They were made to take an oath to observe the five Ks, namely hair (Kesh); comb (Kangha); steel bangle (Kara) on the right wrist; sword (Kirpan) and knee long drawers (Kuchha). They were also to observe the four rules of conduct: not to cut their hair; not to eat *halal* (animal slaughtered in the Muslim fashion) meat; not to smoke, chew tobacco or consume alcoholic beverages and lastly not to violate the modesty of any women (even the enemy's). After baptizing the five, Guru Gobind Singh was in turn baptized by them. The poet subsequently sang, "*Wah Wah!* Guru Gobind Singh *Appe Gur-Chela.*" (Guru Gobind Singh was hailed as himself being Master as well as disciple). He was no longer their superior, but had merged his entity in the Khalsa. At the end of the ceremony they hailed each other with the new greeting – *Wah Guru Ji ka Khalsa – Wah Guru Ji ke Fateh* – The Khalsa is the chosen of God – Victory is to God. On the first day about twenty thousand men came into the fold and according to one estimate as many as eighty thousand (80,000) Sikhs were initiated in a few days. It was now left to Guru Gobind Singh to teach the Khalsa the use of arms as well as to convince them of the morality of the use of force.

Many historians feel that there were four pertinent considerations for the creation of the Khalsa by Guru Gobind Singh. The first and foremost was the atrocities of the Mughals (especially Aurangzeb) and Muslims. The second was the internal condition of Sikhism. The *Masand* system had become totally corrupt. Disunity and decadence had crept into the movement launched by Guru Nanak and there were squabbles over the succession to the guruship. The third was the caste system which was a stumbling block in the way of unity and brotherhood among the Hindus. Lastly there were many Jats among the Sikhs who were brave and loved adventure and warfare. They preferred the sword to the rosary. The creation of the Khalsa was in consonance with their taste and nature. They had to be kept within the fold, for the chosen path to be followed. Henceforth they were needed for the military operations and turbulent times that were imminent.

On close scrutiny, it is found that the main aim of the entire exercise was to obliterate all distinctions of caste, creed and religion and to follow one creed and one path. The other aims would automatically take care of themselves. The Khalsa was to adopt the way of cooperation, mix freely with one another and no one was to deem himself superior to another. They were to receive baptism, eat out of the same vessel, and feel no disgust or contempt for one another. Guru Gobind's motto was: *manas ke jaat sab ek he pahchanbo* – recognize all mankind as one caste. Making people drink *amrit* out of a common bowl (the orthodox Hindu practice considered food or drink touched by a lower caste as polluted) was to break through the orthodox caste system. Similarly the giving of the name 'Singh' or lion (current among Hindu martial classes) to all men and '*Kaur*' or lioness/ princess to all women instead of their surnames (it gives a person's caste) was a step in the same direction. The common name identifies each person as a part of the community, as part of the same family, and as willing to fight for the faith.

Sikhism had already done away with caste and the institution of Langar and Sewa were deeply embedded, however it was left to Guru Gobind Singh to further strengthen and amalgamate them. Thus the phrase '*Deg Teg Fateh*' came in vogue. *Deg* means a cauldron/kettle/kitchen -- to feed the poor and needy. *Teg* means a sword -- a symbol of freedom and sovereignty and the protector of the weak and helpless. And *Fateh* means victory. Thus it means **Prosperity in Peace and Victory in War** or in other words it literally means **'May our charity and our arms be victorious.'** Charity and wielding of the sword for a just cause hold a special place in the Sikh Faith. Charity is the greatest gift that saveth life. The Guru said, "He, who serves the poor and needy, serves me. The mouth of the poor and hungry is the Guru's receptacle of gifts - (*Graib da Munh Guru Ki Golakh*)." The Sword eradicates oppression and tyranny and establishes righteousness. **These two things contributed the most to the popularity and power of the Sikhs and their church.** Ideologically, the Khalsa aimed at a balanced combination of the ideals of *bhagti* and *Shakti*, or to express in modern terminology: the

Khalsa was to be a brotherhood in faith and a brotherhood in arms at one and the same time. All this was an absolute must in order to forge a sect of pacifists into a militant brotherhood of crusaders – 'saint-soldiers' (*sant-sepahi*). It was mandatory for the unity and solidarity of the Khalsa fraternity. It was a historical need - a predominant and urgent demand of the times.

> The Sikhs implicitly believed that:
>
> The Khalsa shall rule.
>
> Their enemies (non believers) will be scattered.
>
> Only they that seek refuge will be saved.

Before proceeding further it would be worthwhile to explore the meaning of the word Khalsa. Khalsa is an Arabic word. It stands for the land that belongs to the king and not to an individual. It means **crown-lands** administered directly by the king or lands directly under government management. Till some time back this word was commonly used in maintaining revenue records in Indian languages. The 6th and 9th Gurus have addressed the Sikh *sangat* as Khalsa in their *Hukamnamahs* (epistle). The word occurs once in the Sikh scriptures. The word Khalsa is used here for the fearless worshippers of God almighty. On page 655 of the Guru Granth Sahib Bhagat Sheikh Kabir in his couplet says, those slaves of God who love to worship Him have become Khalsa.

> Kaho Kabir jan bhaiye Khalse prem bhagat jih jaani.

Khalsa is a Persio-Turkish administrative term, which means royal, not subordinate to anyone, answerable to none subordinate, sovereign, directly administered by the Sovereign. To interpret the meaning of Khalsa as pure is to create a division from other non-Sikh people. Thus the literal meaning of the word Khalsa would be **sovereign.**

The creation of the new order (Khalsa) had manifold ramifications. It caused a great stir, while some embraced the order of the Khalsa readily, others were reluctant. They found the code too tough and incompatible with family traditions and customs. The situation led to dissensions among Sikhs and tension between Sikhs and non-Sikhs. The higher castes, by and large remained aloof. Some of them professed that they had faith in the religion of Sri Guru Nanak Dev and other Gurus, but refused to adopt the 5 Ks and change to the new order. Those who did not accept the changes brought about by Guru Gobind Singh began thereafter to be addressed as *Sahaj Dhari* (those who take time to change or those who take it easy or slow adopters) Sikhs as opposed to the *Singh/Kesh Dhari/Amrit Dhari/Khalsa* Sikhs. Later the British called them the Sikhs of Nanak and the Sikhs of Gobind. Thus not all Sikhs belong to the Khalsa order.

The Khalsa leadership, therefore, came to be comprised mostly of those who from the time of Manu had been denied any respectable status in the Varna based Hindu society. Since the Khalsa order repudiated caste and other distinctions on the basis of wealth, profession, culture, creed, etc. Jats and other socially neglected classes rejoiced, and the Khalsa movement became synonymous with the rise of hereto neglected classes/groups/individuals. It was observed that even those people who had been dregs of humanity were changed, as if by magic into something rich and strange. The sweepers, barbers and confectioners who had never touched a sword, and whose ancestors had lived as groveling slaves of the so-called higher classes, became doughty warriors under the stimulating leadership of Guru Gobind Singh. They never shrank from fear, and were ready to jump into the jaws of death at the bidding of the Guru. The character and development of the Sikh movement had three main social goals: (a) create an egalitarian society. (b) Use the new society as a base to wage an armed struggle against religious and political oppression and (c) seize political power for the Khalsa. These aims were an integral part of Sikh thesis and ethos that injustice, inequality and hierarchism, in whatsoever form must be always combated everywhere and every time.

Nowhere has Guru Gobind Singh given the how and why of the significance of the Five Ks. Perhaps after the baptism ceremony, the turbulent period that followed did not give him much time. But they are not very difficult to understand. The Five Ks are a set of five distinctive features or elements of personal appearance or apparel that set the Sikhs apart (give a separate identity) from the followers of any other religious faith. Since they all start with the letter K, hence the name Five Ks.

Kesh or unshorn hair imprints on the individual the investiture of the spiritual man exemplified in Hinduism by *rishis* or sages and even of God Himself (whose epithet *keshava* means one who carries long tresses). *Kesh* also signify strength (Samson in the Bible), manliness, virility, courage and dignity, and therefore signify qualities both of a *sant* (saint) and a *sipahi* (soldier) and a life both of *bhakti* (spiritual devotion) and *Shakti,* i.e. strength of conviction, of courage, and of fortitude. Keeping the times and conditions in view, it was more convenient and made a man look fierce, intimidating and brave as a lion in battle.

Sometimes long scientific explanations of the advantages of full grown hair are advanced, which are really not needed. It is enough to say that the Sikhs keep their hair untrimmed and uncut first because it is one of their religious vows and secondly because it is a clear mark of **identification**. The other four emblems are complimentary to this one and the profession of soldering.

Kangha (the small comb required to keep the hair tidy) symbolizes cleanliness. As a vestured symbol, it appears to **repudiate** the practice of keeping the hair matted. The *kangha* is a small comb stuck in the chignon on top of the head and the turban tied over it. Thus it becomes a part and parcel of the body and is carried on the hair at all times. Hence it is handy whenever and wherever time permitted its use and requirement.

Kirpan (the sword) signifies valour. For Guru Gobind Singh the sword was the emblem of divine energy for the destruction of the evil and protection of the good. It is also called *bhagauti* (*bhagvati* or the goddess Durga, slayer of the demons) which in Sikh vocabulary stands for the sword as well as for the Almighty. The sword is considered synonymous with God. The sword is also a symbol of freedom and sovereignty. Unlike a dagger, which is a weapon of clandestine attack, the sword is a weapon of open combat. The *kirpan* is a symbol of active resistance against evil. The word *kirpan* seems to have been compounded from *kirpa* (compassion) and *an* (honour, dignity). Hence as a symbolic weapon it shall only be wielded in compassion (to protect the oppressed) and for upholding righteousness and human dignity. It stands therefore, for the heroic affirmation of honour and valour for the vindication of ethical principles. In praise of the sword Guru Gobind Singh says:

> "Sword, that smiteth in a flash,
> That scatters the armies of the wicked
> In the great battlefield;
> O thou symbol of the brave,
> Thine arm is irresistible, thy brightness shineth forth
> Thy blaze and splendour dazzling like the sun.
> Sword thou-art the protector of the saints,

> Thou art the scourge of the wicked;
> Scatterer of sinners; I take refuge in thee
> Hail to the Creator, Saviour and Sustainer,
> Hail Thee: Sword Supreme."

Kara (the steel bangle) was adopted as a pragmatic accessory to the *kirpan*. A set of strong steel bangles used to be worn by warriors as protective armour over the arm that wielded the sword. But besides the pragmatic self defense value, it has a deeper symbolic significance. As a circle it signifies perfection, without beginning, without end. Traditionally, a circle also represents dharma, the Supreme Law, and Divine Justice. It also symbolizes restraint and control. The *Kara*, therefore, symbolizes for the Sikhs a just and lawful life of self-discipline (*rahit*) and self-control (*sanjam*).

kachchh (pair of long shorts) As a pragmatic explanation, its sartorial design makes for greater agility and easy movements, thereby ensuring ready preparedness, *tayyar bar tayyar*, (readiness beyond ordinary readiness). It also served as a horseman's riding breeches. This garment ensured agility and was adapted to the horse. It was a fighting man's uniform of those times. As a symbol it also signifies manly control.

In those tumultuous times the Sikhs lived in jungles as outlaws. The Mughal governors were part of an evil and brutal regime and butchers of the Khalsa. The Sikhs were hunted and a price lay on their heads. Their only fault being that they were Sikhs. This persecution lasted for well over a century and a half (from the early seventeenth century to three quarters of the eighteenth century). In these trying times, the five Ks formed a part and parcel of the body of a Khalsa; he ate, slept and moved with them always -- every time and everywhere. This was an added asset for it enabled the Khalsa to be ever ready for action, whenever and wherever the need arose, whether it was to fight, flee or protect, when surprised. The greatest advantage was that the Khalsa being forever prepared, light equipped, and self-contained was thus unencumbered and always ready to act. He could not afford the luxury of hesitation for delay spelled disaster.

The Five Ks made the Khalsa conspicuous and easily recognizable. They stood out from a distance and had no means to deny their identity. It is also likely that, by making his followers easily identifiable by virtue of their outward symbols (turbans and beards), the Guru wanted to create a race that would not be able to deny its religion when in danger but whose external appearance would invite persecution and in turn breed fearlessness, strength and courage to resist it. When besieged, they knew that the enemy would give them no quarter, so they had to either fight to the finish or emerge victorious. Capture would mean a disgraceful and ignoble change of faith or a brutal and cruel death. With the end result vividly evident to them, the choice lay between victory and death (Do or Die). This was the greatest quality that made them fearless and ferocious fighters.

Sun Tzu in his book *The Art of War* says, "Soldiers when in desperate straits lose the sense of fear. If there is no place for refuge, they will stand firm." And again, "Throw your soldiers into positions whence there is no escape, and they will prefer death to flight, officers and men alike will put forth their uttermost strength."

The purpose of the formation of the Khalsa and the Five K's had been to choose five men of tested courage and loyalty to constitute the nucleus of the new order, the Khalsa. Guru Gobind Singh was seeking to infuse into a somewhat disorganized band of followers a spirit of unity, courage and discipline. And nor can we doubt the tremendous influence which it has exercised in the moulding of the Sikh character. Khalsa is an order of 'soldier saints' dedicated to both piety and justice, and pursuing both with a determination, which when necessity compels, may involve the use of the sword. This is the Khalsa ideal and much that we find in subsequent Sikh history is an obvious response to this ideal.

In retrospect it can be aptly concluded that the five Ks were a fighting man's (soldier's) need and uniform of those stormy times. They were a necessity for fighting, easy movement and agility; by becoming an integral part of the body they made a man ever ready for action. Above all, the five Ks were very much essential for identity of the Khalsa and were a paramount and emergent requirement against the atrocities of a monstrous and savage regime, before the whole of north India was made to forcibly adopt the faith of the Arabian prophet. The Khalsa and the 5Ks were an imperative and indispensible need to preserve Hinduism and stem the tide of the onslaught of Islam. It was in fact sine qua non – a thing that is absolutely necessary.

The only change Guru Gobind Singh brought in religion was to expose the other side of the medal. Whereas Nanak had propagated goodness, Guru Gobind condemned evil. One preached the love of one's neighbour, the other the punishment of transgressors. Nanak's God loved His saints; Gobind's God destroyed His enemies. (A History of the Sikhs Vol.1 Page 88 by Khushwant Singh). By creating the Khalsa Guru Gobind Singh defied the might of the Mughal Empire. He had to fight against heavy odds and he sacrificed his father, mother, four sons, thousands of Sikhs and ultimately himself. What greater sacrifice can there be. True Guru Gobind Singh did not leave his followers a kingdom; but he laid the foundation of the Sikh military might by setting up a tradition of reckless valour which became a distinguishing feature of Sikh soldiery. They came to believe in the triumph of their cause as an article of faith, and like their guru asked for no nobler end than death on the battle field.

With clasped hands this boon I crave
When time comes to end my life
Let me fall in mighty strife.

Exactly a hundred years after Guru Gobind Singh's call to arms in 1699, the Sikh Kingdom was founded in 1799 by Maharaja Ranjit Singh.

SRI GURU GRANTH SAHIB (SGGS)

Sri Guru Granth Sahib (SGGS). [Guru (GU=darkness and Ru = dispeller, so it means **Dispeller of darkness** or in other words **spiritual teacher)**; *Granth*=book or volume; Sahib (master or lord) and *Sri* being honorifics] is the name by which the holy book of the Sikhs is commonly known. Another variation of the title is Adi Granth (*adi* means literally, original, first or primary), distinguishing it from the other sacred book of the Sikhs, the *Dasam Granth*, the book of the Tenth Master (Guru Gobind Singh).

The sacred volume was compiled by Bhai Gurdas (1551-1636), the nephew of Guru Amar Das under the directions of Guru Arjun (1563-1606). The *Granth* was transcribed on 01 August 1604 and installed in the Harimander Sahib (Golden Temple) on 16 August 1604. Baba Buddha (1506-1631) was appointed the first *granthi* or high priest. Later in 1706, at Talwandi Sabo, Guru Gobind Singh with the assistance of Bhai Mani Singh as scribe gave final shape to the Guru Granth by incorporating the writings of his father (Guru Tegh Bahadur) in it. The only writing of Guru Gobind Singh in the Guru Granth is perhaps an addition of two lines to a verse by his father on page 1429. Before his death Guru Gobind Singh bestowed the Guruship on Guru Granth Sahib on 07 Oct. 1708, thus completing a process which had been developing for well over a century. Henceforth, the Sikhs were to seek guidance from Guru Granth Sahib. An interesting fact is that Guru Gobind Singh never visited Amritsar.

Guru Granth Sahib has **1430 pages** and comprises writings of six (06) Gurus (1-5 and 9), fifteen (15) Bhagats, eleven (11) Bhatts and four (04) Sikhs, making it a total of **thirty-six (36)**. Adi Granth is unique among the world's scriptures in its inclusion of non-Sikh hymns. Hindu and Muslim writings are included in what is called the *Bhagat*

Bani. It comprises about one-sixth of the total (938 *sabads* out of a total of 5834), thus exceeding the contribution of any one Guru other than Guru Arjun.

From the list below, it will be apparent that out of the list of 36 individuals whose writings are incorporated in the Guru Granth there are writings of seven (07) Muslim saints (Farid, Kabir, Sadhna, Bikhan, Mardana, Satta and Balwand). The saints or holy men represent a cross section of the caste hierarchy as well as social strata and geographical distribution. The Gurus recognized no distinction of any kind whatsoever. The sole criterion in the selection of hymns was congruence with the universal philosophy preached by Guru Nanak.

The total number of hymns attributed to the writers of Guru Granth is:

<u>Gurus</u>

> Guru Nanak - 974
>
> Guru Angad - 62
>
> Guru Amar Das - 907
>
> Guru Ram Das - 679
>
> Guru Arjan - 2,218
>
> Guru Teg Bahadur - 116

<u>Bhagats</u>

1. Kabir - (1440-1518) a Muslim weaver from UP - 541

2. Farid - a Muslim Sufi saint from Pak Pattan (Punjab now in Pakistan) - 116

3. Namdev - a tailor from Maharashtra - 60

4. Ravidas - a cobbler (*Chamar*) from UP - 41

Slight variations upon these figures may be found in some books as some passages (e.g. the Epilogue of the Japji and pages 08 to 13 occur in more than one place and may be counted twice). The *shloks* of Baba Fraid which are to be found on pages 1377 to 1384 provide a specific example of the enumeration and attribution. Eighteen (18) of the *shloks* are not his, though some authorities assign them to Fraid and therefore give the total as 134 hymns [including four (04) hymns found elsewhere]. So the total count is 116 hymns and not 134 as given in many books. (Reference - The Sikhs by W. Owen Cole and Piara Singh Sambhi).

The other eleven *Bhagats* have one (01) to four (04) hymns and the location of these in Adi Granth is as follows:

5. Jaidev -- a Bengali Brahamin poet - 02 (page 526 - 01 and page 1106 - 01).

6. Trilochan – a *Vahish* from Maharashtra – 04 (page 92 - 01, page 525 - 02 and page 695 - 01).

7. Sadhna – a Muslim butcher from Sindh – 01 (page 858).

8. Beni – perhaps from Punjab (no other details are known) – 03 (page 93 - 01, page 974 - 01 and page 1351 - 01).

9. Ramanand – a Brahamin from Tamil Naidu – 01 (page 1195).

10. Pipa – a Rajput king from Rajasthan – 01 (page 695).

11. Sain – a barber from Rewa MP – 01 (page 695).

12. Dhanna – a Jat (farmer) from Rajasthan – 03 (page 487 - 01, page 488 - 01 and page 695 - 01).

13. Bikhan – a Muslim Sufi saint from UP – 02 (page 659 - 02).

14. Parmanand – a Brahamin from Maharashtra – 01 (page-1253).

15. Surdas – a Brahamin from UP – one line on page 1253.

Four Sikhs*

Satta and Balwand – the two Muslim brothers were rababis or rebeck-players (*mirasis*) in the court of Guru Arjan – 08 (page 966 - 03 and page 968 - 05).

Sundar – was the great grandson of Guru Amar Das. His father, Anand Das was the son of Baba Mohri – 06 (pages 923 and 924).

Mardana – a Muslim *mirasi* was the constant companion of Guru Nanak – 03 on page 553.

Pages 1389 to 1409 contain compositions known as *Swayyas* of the eleven (11) Bhatts (musicians) at Guru Arjan's court.

- Of the non-Sikh contributors Kabir is one who stands nearest to Guru Nanak in his teachings and has most *sabads* included in Adi Granth (541). He is considered to be nominally a Muslim, although his thoughts were Hindu. Islamic thought has little place in his ideas. 'Ram' is the name which he commonly uses to describe God, but like Guru Nanak, the saint tradition of North India is his spiritual context rather than *Vaishnavism* or Islam. Kabir was critical of both Hinduism and Islam for meaningless rites and mindless repetitions. From Hinduism Kabir accepted the ideas of reincarnation and the law of Karma but rejected idolatry, asceticism, and caste system. From Islam he accepted the ideas of one God and equality of all men. Revered by Hindus and Muslims alike, he is also considered a forerunner of Sikhism. He preached humanity and equality, of the Quran and *Puranas*, Ram and Rahim, Krishna and Karim.

- In the 17th century there can be no doubt that Ramanand was the most important of pre-Nanak saints, being regarded as the Guru, not only of Kabir, but of Raidas, Sain, Pipa and Dhanna. These poets, who are also represented in Adi Granth, are numbered among his twelve (12) most important missionary disciples. He belonged to the school of Ramanuja, the founder of Vasistadvaita. Ramananda had liberal views regarding caste distinctions in general and untouchability in particular. His links with these low caste disciples may be evidence of a 16th century attempt to tie these sects into the main stream of *Vaishnavite bhakti* by giving them a famous Brahmin as their Adi-Guru. In his single hymn in the Guru Granth (pg 1195) idol-worship is clearly rejected, the supreme Deity, Brahman, is conceived as all-pervading, revealed to the mind only through the *sabda* of the True Guru, whereas *Vedas* and *Puranas* avail nothing.

- The number of verses in the SGGS varies from 5871 to 5894 according to various scholars. This difference is due to different methods adopted while counting. Otherwise, there is no scope for any difference as the number of pages stand fixed at 1430 and no one is allowed to include or exclude even a letter. The slight variations are due to some passages e.g. the Epilogue of the Japji and pages 08 to 13 occur in more than one place and may be counted twice. The Fraid *Bani* (verses) presents something of a problem because some may be by the famous Chisti's successors rather than the original head of the orders centred at Pak Pattan in Punjab. Thus they might similarly represent a school rather than an individual. 'Fraid' was certainly the name of the *pir* of Pak Pattan when Guru Nanak visited it.

- The *Mirasis* were a caste of hereditary minstrels and genealogists and had served the house of the Gurus (16th-17th centuries) as *rabab* players, hence, called *rababis*. Most of them were Muslim and except

Sheikh Farid, all of them (Mardana, Satta and Balwand) came from the lower strata of society.

- Compositions called *swayye* of eleven contemporary bards called Bhatt (16th century) are included in SGGS. The Bhatts were hereditary Brahmin bards and genealogists. They frequented the courts of princes and camps of warriors, recited their praises and kept records of their genealogies. These bards constantly attended upon or visited their patron families reciting panegyrics and receiving customary rewards. They also collected information about births, deaths and marriages in the families and recorded it in their scrolls called *vahis*. On the whole, these Bhatt–*Vahis* are a mine of information. Some of these Bhatts came into the Sikh fold. There are differences among scholars as to the names and number of Bhatts whose compositions are included in SGGS, which range from eight (08) to seventeen (17). The consensus however is on eleven, as their number.

- Barring pages 1 to 13 (containing important hymns which Sikhs use in daily meditation) and the last 78 pages (that contain hymns which are often so short that they could not be placed in the main body of the text satisfactorily), the rest of the book is divided into thirty-one (31) parts. Each part is made according to Indian musical measures called ragas to which it should be sung. The hymns of the *Granth* are not arranged by authors or subject matter but divided into 31 *ragas* or musical modes in which they are meant to be sung. Thus the SGGS can be sung to musical measures or *ragas*.

- All the Gurus used the word 'O Nanak' in their hymns and were it not for Guru Arjan assigning the various contributions to Nanak 1, Nanak

2 and so on, it would have been impossible to distinguish between them.

- Number of times the words '*Hari*', 'Ram' and '*Wahe Guru*' occur among the 15,028 names of God mentioned in Adi Granth is 8,000, 2,533 and 16 respectively.

- The first two English versions or translations of SGGS were by Gopal Singh and Manmohan Singh. Today many English versions and translations in many other languages are available.

- The Spanish translation of Sri Guru Granth Sahib was uploaded on Sikhitothemax website (Sevatothemax [U.K.], Nov. 07, 2008, 12:44 PM).

- The first published translation of Guru Granth Sahib into Sindhi was done in 1959 by Mr. Jethanand B. Lalwani and published by Bharat Jivan Publications. He used his entire personal savings and was able to produce only 500 copies. Lalwani later took out loans to make a reprint in 1963.

- Dada Lachman Chellaram has printed Sri Guru Granth Sahib in Arabic Sindhi and Devnagri Script in multicolours and at present the same work in *Devnagri* and *Gurmukhi* scripts are under print. He has also translated Sri Guru Granth Sahib in Sindhi and Hindi. Besides, at present, he is busy in bringing out the translation of Sri *Dasam Granth* Sahib in Hindi in 4 volumes. His many audio and video cassettes and CDs of *Kirtan* are in great demand around the world along with his publications.

Sri Guru Granth Sahib is the means and not the object of worship. The main appeal of the *Granth* as a scripture is its non-esoteric character and its utter simplicity.

*In Sikh parlance they are called Sikhs because they were followers of the Gurus. Sikhism is an eclectic religion. It is liberal, catholic and generous and does not believe in proselytizing. So there was no need to change names or ways of people, unless they themselves wanted to do so. Moreover the times and conditions were such.

PRAISE OF SRI GURU GRANTH SAHIB BY SOME MODERN SCHOLARS

The Sikh scriptures are unique among the religious Holy Books of the world in that they don't just offer spiritual guidance for the Sikhs alone but impart guidance and assistance for all people and religions of the world.

Sri Guru Granth Sahib is a supreme treasure for all mankind. It is the true and permanent spiritual guide of the Sikhs. Guru Granth Sahib transcends creed and caste, cant and convention. It does not belong to the Sikhs alone. It consecrates the sayings of 11 Hindu *bhagats*, many bards and 7 Muslim saints, along with the teachings of 6 Sikh gurus. No other religion has included in its holy book the sayings of others, however revered. The Guru Granth Sahib provides unique and unequalled guidance and advice to the whole human race. It is the torch that will lead humanity out of *Kalyug*, (the dark era) to a life in peace, tranquility and spiritual enlightenment for all the nations of the World.

Rev. H. L. Bradshaw of the U.S.A., Sikh Review, Calcutta.

Sikhism is a universal world Faith.....A message for all men. This is amply illustrated in the writings of the Gurus.

Sikhs must cease to think of their faith as just another religion and must begin to think of Sikhism being the religion for this New Age.

He also adds:

"The Guru Granth Sahib of all the world religious scriptures, alone states that there are innumerable worlds and universes other than our own. The previous scriptures were all concerned only with this world and its spiritual counterpart. To imply that they spoke of other worlds as does the Guru Granth Sahib is to stretch their obvious meanings out of context. The Sikh religion is truly the answer to the problems of the modern man."

Miss Pearl S. Buck, a Nobel Laureate

(From the foreword to the English translation of Sri Guru Granth Sahib by Dr Gopal Singh Dardi)

Miss Pearl S. Buck, a Nobel laureate wrote: "When I was in India in 1962, one of the notable events of my visit was the presentation to me of the English version of Sri Guru-Granth Sahib, translated and annotated by Dr. Gopal Singh. I was deeply grateful to receive this great work, for in the original it was inaccessible to me, and this was a matter of regret, for I have had many Sikh friends, and have always admired their qualities of character. Now that I have had time in my quiet Pennsylvania home to read their scriptures slowly and thoughtfully, I can understand why I have found so much to admire. The religion of a people has a profound and subtle influence upon them as a whole, and this is true whether individuals do or do not profess to be religious."

"I have studied the scriptures of the great religions, but I do not find elsewhere the same power of appeal to the heart and mind as I find here in these volumes. They are compact in spite of their length and are a revelation of the concept of God to the recognition and indeed the insistence upon the practical needs of the human body. There is something strangely modern about these scriptures and this puzzled me until I learned that they are in fact comparatively modern, compiled as late as the 16th century when explorers were beginning to discover the globe upon which we all live is a single entity divided only by arbitrary lines of our making. Perhaps this sense of unity is the source of power I find in these volumes. They speak to a person of any religion or of none. They speak for the human heart and the searching mind."

Archer in his book on Sikh faith:

The religion of the Guru Granth is a universal and practical religion…Due to ancient prejudices of the Sikhs it could not spread in the world. The world needs today its message of peace and love.

Dorothy Field in her book, The Sikh Religion:

"Pure Sikhism is far above dependence on Hindu rituals and is capable of a distinct position as a world religion so long as Sikhs maintain their distinctiveness. The religion is also one which should appeal to the occidental mind. It is essentially a practical religion. If judged from the pragmatic standpoint which is a favorite point of view in some quarters, it would rank almost first in the world (emphasis by the author). Of no other religion can it be said that it has made a nation in so short a time."

She also adds:

"The religion of the Sikhs is one of the most interesting at present existing in India, possibly indeed in the whole world. A reading of the Granth strongly suggests that Sikhism should be regarded as a new and separate world religion rather than a reformed sect of Hinduism."

Arnold Toynbee, a historian

Main article: Arnold Toynbee

Arnold Joseph Toynbee (1889 – 1975) was a British historian whose twelve-volume analysis of the rise and fall of civilizations, A Study of History, 1934-1961, was a synthesis of world history, a meta - history based on universal rhythms of rise, flowering and decline, which examined history from a global perspective. His work includes over 50 titles on various aspects of world history.

Toynbee has given a very high and prominent place to Sri Guru Gobind Singh *Ji* in Sikh History. He calls Guru *Ji* a *"divinity of highest rank."* He gets emotional when he writes about Guru Sahib's contribution in the formation of Khalsa. Again and again he emphasizes the fact that there cannot be any person like the Sikh Gurus.

(Foreword to the Sacred Writings of the Sikhs by UNESCO)

Mankind's religious future may be obscure; yet one thing can be foreseen. The living higher religions are going to influence each other more than ever before, in the days of increasing communications between all parts of the world and branches of human race. In this coming religious debate, the Sikh religion and its scriptures, the Guru Granth, will have something special of value to say to the rest of the world.

Dr. W.O Cole of U.K.

He has written more than half a dozen books on Sikhism. In 1985, he visited India where in a keynote lecture by him on the Mission and Message of Guru Nanak Dev, he gave a message to the *Sangat* there and through them to all of humanity:

Remember the tenets of Guru Nanak, his concepts of oneness of God and Universal Brotherhood of man. If any community holds the key to national integration of India, it is the Sikhs all the way.

After the lecture, he was asked what drew him to the study of Sikhism. (Quoted from Spokesman, Toronto, Canada) He replied:

Theologically, I cannot answer the question what drew me to the study of Sikhism. You may call it, the purpose of God. But to be more specific, the unique concept of universality and the system of *Langar* (free community meal) in Sikhism are the two features that attract me towards the study of Sikhism. *Langar* is the exclusive feature of Sikhism and found nowhere else in the world. Sikhism is the only religion which welcomes each and every one to its *langar* without any discrimination of caste, creed, color, or sex.

Swami Nitya Nand

A Hindu mystic mentions his experiences with the Sikh faith. (He is believed to have expired at the age of 135 years). He writes in his book "Gur Gian":

I, in the company of my guru, Brahma Nand Ji, went to Mathura…While on pilgrimage tour, we reached Punjab and here we met Swami Satya Nand Udasi. He explained the philosophy and religious practices of Nanak in such a way that Swami Brahma Nand Ji enjoyed a mystic lore. During the visit to the Golden Temple, Amritsar, his soul was so much affected that he became a devotee of the Guru. After spending some time in Punjab he went to Hardwar. Though he was hale and hearty, one day I saw tears in his eyes. I asked the reason for that.

He replied, "I sifted sand the whole of my life. The truth was in the house of Nanak. I will have to take one more birth in that house, only then will I attain *Kalyan*."

After saying that the soul left his body.

Swami Nitya Nand also wrote his own experience:

I also constantly meditate on *Waheguru* revealed by Nanak. I practiced Yoga *Asanas* under the guidance of Yogis and did that for many years; the bliss and peace which I enjoy now was never obtained earlier.

President George W. Bush

Our Nation has always benefited from a strong tradition of faith, and religious diversity has been an important part of this heritage. The Guru Granth Sahib has provided strength, wisdom, and guidance to hundreds of thousands of Sikhs in America and millions more around the world.

I applaud the Sikh community for your compassion and dedication to your faith. By sharing its message of peace, equality, and the importance of family, you help change lives, one heart and one soul at a time. Bush added Laura (Bush's wife) joins me in sending our best wishes.

Authenticity of Guru Granth Sahib

This is what **Max Arthur Macauliffe** writes about the authenticity of the Guru's teaching:

"The Sikh religion differs as regards the authenticity of its dogmas from most other theological systems. Many of the great teachers the world has known have not left a line of their own composition and we only know what they taught through tradition or second-hand information. If Pythagoras wrote of his tenets, his writings have not descended to us. We know the teachings of Socrates only through the writings of Plato and Xenophanes. Buddha has left no written memorial of his teaching. Kungfu-tze, known to Europeans as Confucius, left no documents in which he detailed the principles of his moral and social system. The founder of Christianity did not reduce his doctrines to writing and for them we are obliged to trust to the gospels according to Matthew, Mark, Luke and John. The Arabian Prophet did not himself reduce to writing the chapters of the Quran. They were written or compiled by his adherents and followers. But the compositions of Sikh Gurus are preserved and we know at firsthand what they taught."

Bertrand Russel on Sri Guru Granth Sahib and Sikhism

Jugojug atall dharm ka jaikar bolo ji waheguru!!

Bertrand Russel 1950, Russell was awarded the **Nobel Prize in Literature** he said, "If some lucky men survive the onslaught of the third world war of atomic and hydrogen bombs, the **SIKH** religion will be the **ONLY** means of guiding them. It has the capacity, but **Sikhs** have not brought-out, in broad day light, the splendid doctrine of their religion, which has come into existence for the b**enefit of entire mankind**."

 Western Atheist's Views

We were doing great with knocking out Christianity, Judaism, Islam, Hinduism, Baha'i, even Buddhism but we have gotten very stuck with Sikhism.

.... Look instead in service to humanity. You will find "meaning" in your love for other human beings. You can experience God when you help someone who needs your help.

Why is this interesting? Because we found this religion of Sikhism to be in agreement with this! This is why we have a problem. We tried to look at their holy text (Adi Granth) but didn't find the usual absurdities we found in the other religious books. In fact it's refreshingly inspiring and very good!

Did you know that they believed in **Democracy, freedom of speech, choice, expression, freedom of religion, pluralism, human rights, equality between men and women, equality of all people regardless of race, religion, caste, creed, status etc.** 300 years before the existence of the USA! Theirs is the <u>only</u> religion which says in their religious scripts that women are equal in every respect to men. They even had women soldiers leading armies in to battle against "you know who" (The usual suspects – Muslims!) Their history is a proud one; they fought in both World Wars. Even Hitler praised them for their bravery and Aryan heritage!

We have been trying for weeks now to find a way to fairly and rationally criticize and find fault with this religion but have failed. We even found out that there are many people converting to this religion in the USA and Europe as well as Russia (Mostly well educated and affluent white people).

Please bear in mind that **Bertrand Russell** was a great philosopher and free thinker and is said to have given Christianity (same applies to Islam and Judaism) a body blow and exposed its absurdities; but even this great man got stuck when it came to Sikhism! In fact he gave up and said **"that if some lucky men survive the onslaught of the third world war of atomic and hydrogen bombs, then the Sikh religion will be the only means of guiding them." Russell was asked that he was talking about the third world war, but isn't this religion capable of guiding mankind before the third world war? In reply, Russell said, "Yes, it has this capability, but the Sikhs have not brought out in the broad daylight, the splendid doctrines of this religion which has come into existence for the benefit of the entire** mankind. This is their greatest sin and the Sikhs cannot be freed of it.

 What Bertrand was most impressed with was that Sikhism does not have a doctrine of evangelism that <u>it does not go out to try to subvert and convert</u>. In some ways he thought that Sikhs should go out and propagate their great faith.

HARIMANDAR SAHIB (GOLDEN TEMPLE)

Harimandar (Lit. the House of God; hari = Vishnu, or God; mandar = temple, house), Golden Temple to the English–speaking world, is the Sikhs' most famous sacred shrine. Also called Sri Darbar Sahib (the Exalted Holy Court), it lies in the heart of the city of Amritsar in Punjab. The city in fact grew around what initially stood as the temple portal. The present structure could well be described as a golden beauty amidst a glittering pool of water.

Work on the holy tank of Amritsar had commenced in AD 1577 by Guru Ram Das (1534-81), on a site which, according to some sources, was purchased during the time of Guru Amar Das (1479-1574), from the inhabitants of the nearby village Tung, and which, according to other sources, was a gift from the Mughal emperor Akbar (1542-1605) to Guru Amar Das's daughter, Bibi Bhani, married to Guru Ram Das. The habitation which developed around the tank first came to be known as Ramdaspur, after the name of Guru Ram Das, or simply as Chakk Guru (the Guru's village). The tank was completed by Guru Arjun, who also raised the structure, Harimandar, in the middle of it. The completion of the temple was consummated with the installation in it, on **16 August 1604,** of the Holy Scripture Sri Guru Granth Sahib.

On the invitation of Guru Arjun, the foundation of the building of Golden Temple was laid by the **Muslim divine saint Hazrat Mian Mir** (1550-1635), of Lahore on **28 December 1588**. Unlike the Hindu custom of having the shrine built on a high plinth level, Guru Arjun had it built on a lower level than the surrounding ground and instead of having one entrance, he had four. It was a sign of humility. The highest and lowest would have to go down even lower, in order to shed their social status, pride and ego and the four doors of the temple, opening in the four cardinal directions signified that God is one and omnipresent and also that the four castes, were all equal, welcome and free to enter. Anyone and everyone who wished to enter were at liberty to do so without any distinction of caste, creed, religion, race, colour, sex or social status. In fact there is no discrimination or bias on any ground whatsoever.

Sri Harimandir Sahib being the source of Sikh life and faith remained the main target of attack during the period of persecution by the Mughal rulers and by Afghan invaders during the eighteenth century. In March-April 1709, the governor of Lahore set up a police post at Amritsar and sent an army contingent to suppress the Sikhs. Despite this the place remained popular and multitudes came thronging to the shrine, especially twice a year on the festivals of *Baiskhi* and *Diwali*. This continued even after the arrest and execution in 1716 of Banda Singh along with a large number of Sikhs. The more the authorities tried to impede the Sikhs from visiting their sacred shrine, the more they defied the ban. Each and every time the Sikhs sacrificed their lives to liberate their shrine and restore its sanctity.

After the martyrdom of Bhai Mani Singh ji[1] in 1737, Massa Ranghar[2], the *Kotwal* of Amritsar took charge of Sri Harimandir Sahib in **1740** and converted it into a civil court and began to hold nautch parties. This act created great resentment among the Sikhs. Two warriors, **Sukha Singh** and **Mahtab Singh** avenged the insult by a dare devil act. On **11 August 1740**, they entered the temple complex in the guise of peasants, severed the head of Massa Ranghar with a single blow of the *kirpan* and fled with the decapitated head on a spear. After this incident the security around Sri Harimandir Sahib was further tightened and the temple was locked.

In **1746 Lakhpat Rai[3]**, a Hindu *Diwan* of Lahore *Darbar* vowed to finish the entire Sikh Nation, in order to avenge the death of his brother Jaspat Rai. He fouled the *Sarovar* and desecrated Sri Harmandir Sahib. He even banned the epithet 'Guru'. The Mughal forces marched against the Sikhs under the command of Diwan Lakhpat Rai and Yahiya Khan. A fierce battle was fought (the first / Chotta Ghalughara or lesser holocaust in June 1746) in which nearly seven thousand Sikhs were martyred. In addition more than a thousand of them were put to death publicly at Lahore (the site is now called Shaheedganj). After this holocaust, the Sikhs under the able leadership of **Sardar Jassa Singh Ahluwalia[4]** retaliated and recaptured both the city and Sri Harimandir Sahib killing Salabat Khan in March, 1748. They celebrated B*aiskhi* with great enthusiasm by cleaning the holy *Sarovar* and restoring the daily *Maryada* (tradition) at Sri Harimandir Sahib. They also held 'Sarbat Khalsa' (biannual meetings at Amritsar on *Baisakhi* and *Diwali* to decide matters concerning the community) and the *Diwali* festival of 1748 was celebrated with gaiety and enthusiasm.

In **1757**, Ahmad Shah Abdali (later Durrani) invaded India for the fourth time and on his return from Delhi with his spoils, attacked

Amritsar. He demolished Sri Harmandir Sahib and desecrated it, defiling the tank by casting into it the waste and entrails of slaughtered cows. The Sikhs wrested control of the shrine, when **Baba Deep Singh ji**[5] Sahaid, the head of 'Misl Shaheedan', on hearing of the desecration, started at once from his abode to avenge the insult. On **11 Nov. 1757** a bloody encounter took place at the village Gohalwar near Amritsar. Baba Deep Singh was mortally wounded. He gripped and supported his almost severed head with his left hand and with the right hand he went on mowing down the enemy. Thus fighting, this great warrior reached the holy precincts and there laid down his life. A memorial in his memory stands at this place today. The Sikhs had the holy tank cleaned by Afghan soldiers captured during the campaign undertaken jointly with Adina Beg, the *faujdar* of Jalandhar Doab, and the Marathas against Ahmad Shah's son, Prince Taimur, and his deputy Jahan Khan.

On **10th April, 1762**, during his sixth invasion, Ahmed Shah Abdali again invaded Amritsar and Sri Harmandir Sahib, after the horrible carnage of the Sikhs at Kup Harira (Vada Ghallughara or the great massacre/ holocaust on **05 February 1762** in which nearly twenty-five to thirty thousand Sikhs were killed). On this occasion thousands of armed and unarmed Sikhs had gathered at the temple for a holy bath. Countless Sikhs laid down their lives in defense of their beloved shrine. Sri Harmandir Sahib was blown up with gun powder and the holy tank was again desecrated. Despite the great holocaust and the mass scale massacre of Sikhs in the preceding spring, by autumn they had regained enough confidence and rallied to return to Amritsar and celebrated the festival of *Diwali* there.

On **01 December, 1764**, Sri Harmandir Sahib was again attacked by Ahmed Shah Abdali during his seventh invasion with the sole object of destroying the entire Sikh Nation. But before his arrival the Sikhs had abandoned the city and what the Afghans saw at the temple gave them some notion of the sort of people they were up against. To his surprise Abdali found only a suicidal squad of thirty Sikhs in the vicinity of Sri Harmandir Sahib, who under the command of **Baba Gurbakhsh Singh ji**[6] gave him stiff resistance and were martyred to the last man. This was the **third time** that Abdali blew up the Harimandir and filled the holy tank with dead cows. Before his final departure from India in 1767, Ahmed Shah Abdali once again took Amrtisar but he dared not attack Sri Harimandir Sahib, perhaps he had been told of the way the Sikhs reacted to defilement of their shrines. Moreover before his arrival the Sikhs had defeated his **General Jahan Khan** and he did not know what to do with a people who would neither fight him in the open nor make friends with him. In spite of all the reverses and slaughters they remained hardened to suffering and defiant to the core and had rebuilt the Harimandir from the debris more than once.

The reconstruction of Harimandar Sahib, the causeway and Darshani Deorhi, the main gateway, was completed by 1776 and the renovation of the terrace around the pool by 1784. The *hansli* or canal bringing water from the River Ravi to fill the Harmandar tank had been dug by 1781 under the supervision of two *Udasi mahants*, Pritam Das and Santokh Das. So the Harimandar Sahib assumed its present appearance and glory during the reign of the Sikh sovereign Maharaja Ranjit Singh (1780-1839). In the early 19th century, 100 kg of gold was used to adorn the inverted lotus-shaped dome and decorative marble was added for its further beautification. All this gold and marble work took place under the patronage of Maharaja Ranjit Singh. The legendary warrior king was a major donor of money and material for the shrine and is remembered with much affection by the Sikh community and Punjabi people. The Shrine remained under the control of the Sikhs thereafter, till **June 1984** when the Golden Temple was attacked by the Indian Army under **Operation Blue Star**.

In June 1984, Indian Prime Minister Indira Gandhi ordered an **attack** on armed Sikh militants holed up in the Golden Temple. Large numbers of people were killed in the ensuing firefight, which included several hundred innocent Sikh pilgrims. Sikhs around the world were outraged at the desecration of their holiest shrine. The Sikh community refused to allow the central government to repair the damage to the temple; instead they undertook the repair work themselves. Although most of the damage has been repaired, the incident has not been forgotten; the wounds of Operation Bluestar will never heal.

After the Martyrdom of Bhai Mani Singh ji, Sri Harimandir Sahib was collectively managed by the Sikh *misls* and many *Bungas* (Mansions) were constructed. Whenever the Sikh leaders visited Amritsar, they did not interfere in the affairs of the temple. All the general gatherings were held in Akal Takhat Sahib only in the presence of Guru Granth Sahib. During the rule of Maharaja Ranjit Singh the administration of Sri Harimandir Sahib went under the control of the State. Maharaja took keen interest in the development and beautification of Sri Harimandir Sahib.

During the British period, Sri Harimandir Sahib passed under the control of one man the '*Sarbrah*' (Manager), a nominee of Deputy Commissioner of Amritsar. The Deputy Commissioner of Amritsar also made a committee of so-called Sikh Sardars and *Raises* (very rich people). The *Pujaries, Mahants, Ragis* and other functionaries began to receive their customary share of offerings at the Temple. On the other hand immoral acts were practiced by them within the precincts of the temple with the connivance of *Sarbrah*. Great resentment prevailed among the Sikhs and this led to the **Sikh Gurdwara Reform Movement**. Again the Sikhs had to sacrifice their lives for the liberation of Sri Harimandir Sahib and other shrines. The Shiromani Akali Dal spear headed the struggle for the reform of the places of worship. The curtain was finally drawn on the Gurdwara Reform Movement, when the Sikh Gurdwara Act, 1925, vested control and management of Sri Harimandir Sahib and other Gurdwaras in the Shiromani Gurdwara Parbandhak Committee, a representative body of the Sikhs elected by adult franchise.

This chapter will be entirely incomplete without a mention of the *Langar*. The *Langar* of the Golden Temple is unique. More than thirty-five thousand people, on an average, partake of the *Langar* daily. On Sundays, holidays, festivals and *Masya* (*Amavas*-no moon day), the gathering exceeds one lakh. At a time, over 3,000 people are served on the two floors of the hall. Everyone is welcome to share the meal, **with no distinction of caste, creed, colour, sex or faith**. It is no ordinary feat to serve a meal to thousands of people **daily and that too round-the-clock**. The power of devotion and *seva* (selfless service) of the *sewadars* and a good number of volunteers, both men and women, who look for no return except *Waheguru's* blessings, makes this arduous task easy and simple to manage. '**IN THY SERVICE**' is their motto. There is division of labour and the whole thing is highly organised -- from arranging the material to cooking and then serving. It is done so meticulously that one is surprised to see all this happen. The kitchen also has a *roti*-making machine, which is however, used only on days that are likely to witness huge crowds. The machine can make *rotis* of 20-kg flour in just half-an-hour. To fetch the flour, there are two machines in the basement of the *langar* hall and another that kneads one quintal of flour in just five minutes.

It is this fine team of man and machine that makes it possible for the gurdwara to provide **24-hour langar on all days**.

About 50-quintal wheat, 18-quintal daal (lentil), 14-quintal rice and seven quintal milk is the daily consumption in the *langar* kitchen. *Desi* Ghee (clarified butter) comes from Verka Milk Plant in the city. The devotees also make donations in cash and kind. In a day, over eight quintals of sugar and an equal quantity of *daal* is received. Besides *dal-roti*, *khee*r and *karah prasad* is prepared on alternate days. On an average, seven quintals of milk and an equal quantity of rice is needed to prepare *kheer*. On festive occasions, *jalebis* (Indian sweet) are also distributed. For making tea, 6 quintals of sugar and 20 kg of tea leaves are consumed. Every day over 100 gas cylinders are needed to fuel the kitchen.

All this wouldn't have been possible without the grace of *Waheguru*: "*Loh langar tapde rahin*" (may the hot plates of the *langar* remain ever in service) are the words that every devotee requests for in his prayers at the gurdwara. The Sikh practice of Guru Ka Langar was strengthened by Guru Amar Das, the third Sikh guru. Even Emperor Akbar, it is said, had to take *langar* with the common people before he could meet Guru Amar Das. *Langar* or community kitchen was designed to uphold the principle of equality between all people regardless of religion, caste, creed, age, colour, gender or social status. In addition to the ideals of equality, the tradition of *langar* also bespeaks of ethics of sharing and oneness of all humankind.

Two Belgian filmmakers, Valerie Berteau and Philippe Witjes were so impressed with the *langar* at the Darbar Sahib that they made a documentary film on it. Entitled 'Golden Kitchen', the film has impressed audiences at numerous film festivals in Europe. On June 6, 2011, it was adjudged 'Outstanding' at the Festival of Short Films organised at the New York Museum of Modern Art. Critics have praised the film for bringing out the beauty of what is for western audiences "an endeavour that is remarkable in scale, the clockwork efficiency with which the kitchen is organised and the fact that all the people manning the kitchen are volunteers who are inspired to undertake the heavy labour by their religious convictions."

In order to summarize, a gist of some facts, already mentioned above and some other interesting ones pertaining to the Golden Temple are given below:

Some Significient, Interesting and Lesser Known Facts of the Golden Temple

The foundation of Harmandir Sahib (Golden Temple) a symbol of brotherhood, equality and glory of the Sikhs was amazingly laid by a Muslim Sufi sage Mian Mir. Its construction was started in 1577 by Guru Ram Das and completed by Guru Arjun Dev in September 1601.

The Golden Temple has four entrances in the North, South, East and West to indicate that God is one and present everywhere. The temple welcomes all people with open arms (to symbolize the openness of the Sikh people towards all other people and religions). People from all walks of life, diverse backgrounds and all four corners of the earth irrespective of caste, creed, colour, faith or wealth are welcome here and permitted to enter and worship. In other words it is open to the entire human race.

Interestingly the Golden Temple is built on a plinth below ground level. It is deliberately built in such a fashion, in order to bring a sense of humbleness and eradicate arrogance of visitors.

Harimandar Sahib was covered with gold by Maharaja Ranjit Singh (the only Sikh ruler ever), almost two centuries after its construction.

Today, the Golden Temple (a <u>famous historical place in India</u>) has become a much sought after destination on the tourist map of India, not only for the Sikh devotees, but also for people from all other parts of the world, without distinction of religion (35% of the people who visit the Golden Temple are non-Sikhs). Taj Mahal attracted 03 million visitors in the whole of 2013. The Golden Temple attracts 03 million visitors in a month. The Golden Temple was ranked No. 06 when BBC's popular holiday programme asked viewers to rank places to see before dying. Taj Mahal was at No.10.

The Golden Temple has been a monument of worldwide fame on account of organizing the largest *langar* (refectory or community kitchen) *sewa* (service) in the world serving more than thirty-five thousand people on an average daily and double and triple this number on special occasions. The Temple served one lakh Jammu and Kashmir victims in September, 2014 by providing food when they needed it most.

After the death of Guru Gobind Singh the Golden Temple was repeatedly attacked, desecrated and destroyed five times by the Mughals. Ahmad Shah Abdali blew it up thrice (1757, 1762 and 1764 during his fourth, sixth and seventh invasions respectively). The temple has been devastated again and again, first by the Mughals and the Afghans and then by the Indian Army in June 1984 on the orders of the prime minister Indra Gandhi during Operation Blue Star. But each time in spite of all the slaughter and suffering the Sikhs rebuilt it at the cost of their lives. This is the kind of reverence; faith and devotion the Sikhs have for their holiest shrine. It is their chief shrine of worship and the most important pilgrimage site of the Sikhs.

In 1757 the Golden Temple was attacked by one of Ahmed Shah Abdali's generals, Jahan Khan. In response a Sikh army hunted down and destroyed Jahan Khan's forces. This battle was fought at village Mahilpur[7] (Hoshiarpur district)

Jahan Khan attacked Amritsar and defiled the sacred pool in the Golden Temple in 1757. To counter him, **seventy-five year old Baba Deep Singh**, the founder of the *Shahid* (martyr) *Misl and* the first head of Damdami Taksal (the Sikh school of learning) gathered a force of 5000 men. The two forces clashed at Gohlvar village, 08 km from Tarn Taran on **11 November 1757**. In the fierce battle that ensued, Deep Singh suffered a mortal injury to his jugular vein near Ramsar. On being reminded of his oath of breathing his last at the Golden Temple he held his almost severed head with one hand and fought his way through with the other to reach the temple and fulfill his vow.

The British Government performed continuous series of *Akhand Paths* (non-stop continuous recital of the Guru Granth Sahib from beginning to end to be completed within 48 hours) at the Golden Temple during the First World War for victory.

On 31 December 1925 a devout Muslim Haji Mohammed Maskin presented an invaluable artifact to the Golden Temple, and carved out a niche for himself for all time to come. The sandalwood *chaur* (whisk) created by Maskin ji is kept in a glass case in the *Toshakhana* (treasure trove) along with other precious items given as gifts to the Temple over the centuries. When the whisk is taken out of the glass box, it fills the environment with the fragrance of sandalwood.

[1]**Bhai Mani Singh** (d. 1737) – was a scholar, martyr and companion of Guru Gobind Singh. He was a pious and venerable head priest and custodian of the Golden Temple. It was with the assistance of Bhai Mani

Singh as a scribe that Guru Gobind Singh gave final shape to the Guru Granth by incorporating the writings of his father (Guru Tegh Bahadur) in it, in 1706, at Talwandi Sabo. Bhai Mani Singh also compiled the Dasam Granth under the guidance of Guru Gobind Singh. In 1737 Zakariya Khan, the governor of Lahore granted him permission to hold the Diwali festival at Amritsar on payment of Rs five thousand as tax. This was a ruse, because on the other hand the governor sent a strong force under Diwan Lakhpat Rai to annihilate the Sikhs, when they would assemble for the festival. Mani Singh came to know of it. So he forbade the Sikhs from leaving their scattered forest and desert abodes to gather at Amritsar. When the tax could not be paid Bhai Mani Singh was given the choice to either embrace Islam or face death. He chose the latter and was executed with his body mangled bone by bone. In Lahore, at the site of his martyrdom, a Gurudwara - Shahid Ganj was constructed. In recent times, another memorial gurdwara has been raised near Longowal, which is believed to be his birthplace.

[2]**Masse Khan Ranghar** (d. 1740), was a Ranghar Rajput landlord, who had converted to Islam. He belonged to village Mandiali, 08 km south of Amritsar. He was appointed *kotwal* of Amritsar by Zakariya Khan, the Mughal governor of Lahore (1726-45), after the death of Qazi Abdur-Rehman, who had met his end at the hands of the Sikhs. Masse Khan's specific charge was not to allow the Sikhs to visit Harimandar Sahib. He stationed himself inside the Harimandar and there he caroused and indulged in revelry with women of ill repute. Most of the fighting bands of Sikhs had already been driven out by Zakariya Khan's drastically harsh measures to seek refuge in the hills and deserts. Massa had a free reign until the news of the sacrilege reached the *jatha* (band) of Sardar Sham Singh camping near Jaipur in Rajasthan. Mahtab Singh and Sukha Singh of this band entered the Golden temple in disguise and beheaded Massa. They then fled with the decapitated head on a spear.

[3]**Lakhpat Rai** (d. 1748), was *diwan* or revenue minister at Lahore, under two successive Mughal governors, Zakarya Khan (1726-45) and his son Yahiya Khan (1745-47). He came from a Hindu *Khatri* family of Kalanaur, in Gurdaspur district of the Punjab. In 1736 Zakariya Khan organized a mobile column of 10,000 soldiers to scour the country side in search of Sikhs, who, were during this period condemned to indiscriminate murder and slaughter of the most inhumane kind. Lakhpat Rai and Mukhlis Khan (the governor's own nephew), were given command of this force. The Sikhs were driven out to take refuge in hills, jungles and the desert. The aim of this move was to establish a reign of terror against the Sikhs in order to annihilate them. They however struck back, off and on, whenever an opportunity came their way. Lakhpat Rai lost his nephew Duni Chand and later his brother Jaspat Rai, while fighting the Sikhs. In 1736 Lakhpat Rai was deputed to proceed to Amritsar in order to molest Sikhs gathering there for the *Diwali* festival, permission for which had been sought by Bhai Mani Singh and granted by the governor himself. It is this incident that led to Bhai Mani Singh's martyrdom and the Sikhs hold Lakhpat Rai wholly and solely responsible for this.

Lakhpat Rai was an avowed enemy of the Sikhs and was determined to wipe them out. He rounded up the Sikh inhabitants of Lahore and carried out a mass execution on Monday, 10 March 1746. Intercession by Diwan Kaura Mal and a group of other prominent Hindus was of no avail. The copies of the Granth Sahib that they found were burned and the tank surrounding the Harimandar Sahib was fouled with rubbish. He and Yahya Khan then set out at the head of a large column, mostly cavalry supported by cannon, in pursuit of Sikhs who were reported to have concentrated in the swampy forest of Kahnuvan on the right bank of River Beas, 15 km south of Gurdaspur. The besieged Sikhs put up a determined fight but being heavily outnumbered, under-equipped and running out of rations were scattered with great losses. More than **seven thousand** Sikhs lost their lives on **01 May 1746.** The matter did not end there; over a thousand were rounded up and brought in chains to Lahore. The captives were paraded, humiliated and disgraced in the streets and then marched to the horse market and publicly slaughtered there. In history this devastation of 01 May 1746 is referred to as the **Chotta Ghallughara** (Minor Holocaust/Massacre) as distinguished from **Vadda Gallughara** (Major Holocaust/Great Massacre) that took place on 05 February 1762. In order to ensure the complete extinction of Sikhs, Lakhpat Rai ordered their places of worship to be destroyed and their holy books burned. He decreed that anyone uttering the word *guru* should have his belly ripped; since the word *gur* (jaggery) sounded like *guru*, he prohibited its use. The Sikhs had five months respite after the *Ghallughara*.

Hereafter the situations changed in quick succession with dramatic suddenness. Shah Nawaz Khan, brother of Yahiya Khan occupied Lahore and imprisoned his brother and Lakhpat Rai; Ahmad Shah Abdali (Durrani) seized Lahore in January 1748 and placed Jalhe Khan as governor with Lakhpat Rai as his *diwan*; the Durrani was defeated by the Mughals and beat a hasty retreat to his country; Mu'in ul-Malik (Mir Manu) became governor and in order to win over the Sikhs appointed a *Sahajdhari* Sikh, Diwan Kaura Mal, as his minister; Kaura Mal procured custody of Lakhpat Rai and handed him over to the Sikhs. Lakhpat Rai was thrown into a dungeon where he died a miserable death.

[4]**Sardar Jassa Singh Ahluwalia** (1718-1783) was founder of the Ahluwalia Misl, remnants of which lasted until recent years in the form of the princely state of Kapurthla. He was born at the village of Ahlu (thus the name), near Lahore on 03 May 1718 and proved his courage and bravery in many a battle. On the *Baisakhi* of 1748, a general assembly of Sikhs (*Sarbat Khalsa*) was convened at Amritsar which

resolved to consolidate the sixty-five roving Sikh *jathas* (bands) into one command called Dal Khalsa under Jassa Singh Ahluwalia. Its eleven (11) subdivisions were called *misls*; the twelfth *misl* Phulkian (House of Patiala) traced a separate origin. Persecution by the Mughal authority under Mir Manu, *subedar* of Lahore (1748 to 1753) had become more virulent.

After the death of Mir Manu in 1753, Jassa Singh started seizing villages and towns that were thrown into confusion by the state of chaos that followed. Like the Maratha *chauth*, he established the system of *rakhi* (protection cess or tax), received for providing protection and security. This is when the use of the word **Sardar** for the Sikhs came in vogue. In April 1754 the Dal Khalsa under the command of Jassa Singh routed an Afghan force from Lahore which had laid siege to Amritsar. In 1757 he struck havoc in the rearguard of Taimur Shah (son of Ahmad Shah) who had been appointed governor of Lahore by his father. In April 1758 on the request of Adina Beg, a combined force of the Sikhs, the Marathas and Adina Beg ransacked Sirhind and then marched into Lahore. Jassa Singh and other *sardars* played a decisive role in reinstalling Adina Beg as the governor of Lahore. After the third battle of Panipat on 17 January 1761 (Ahmad Shah routed the Marathas), the Sikhs under Jassa Singh made a surprise attack on the Shah's force near Amritsar in March 1761 and rescued 2,200 women captives whom the invader was carrying in his train as slaves. In September 1761 a combined force of Jassa Singh and some other Sikh *misls* overpowered the troops of Khwaja Ubaid Khan, Governor of Lahore and then besieged and occupied Lahore. Jassa Singh Ahluwalia was proclaimed as the King of Lahore and he declared the sovereignty of Sikhs. A coin was also issued in the name of Nanak - Guru Gobind Singh to commemorate the Sikh victory with the inscription taken from the seal of Banda Singh Bahadur:

Deg o tegh o fateh o Nusrat be diring

Yaft az Nanak Guru Gobind Singh

(Prosperity, power and unfailing victory received from Nanak and Guru Gobind Singh)

In 1762 Ahmad Shah Abdali or Durrani, on hearing of the fall of Lahore hastened to Punjab. This was his sixth incursion into India. The Sikhs had retired south of the Sutlej and Dal Khalsa lay encamped at **Kup**, 09 km from Malerkotla. In the ensuing battle on **05 February 1762, twenty-five thousand (25, 0000) Sikhs were killed. Jassa Singh sustained twenty-two wounds on his body.** To this day, the Battle of Kup is remembered in Sikh history as **Vadda Ghallughara (Major Holocaust)**. Returning to Lahore, Ahmad Shah marched to Amritsar and had the Holy Harimadar blown up with gunpowder. Under the shadow of the carnage at Kup and the disaster at Amritsar, Jassa Singh with the remains of Dal Khalsa abided his time, awaiting an opportunity to come his way. While the Shah was still at Lahore, he fell upon Sirhind on 17 May 1762 and exalted *nazarana* from Zain Khan, the *faujdar*. The Dal Khalsa under Jassa Singh was active once again. Kathgarh and Garhshankar fell in April 1763; the Afghan commander, Jalan Khan was defeated near Sialkot, in November 1763; Kurali and Morinda were occupied and Sirhind laid waste after the town was attacked on 14 January 1764 and the Afghan faujdar, Zain Khan was slain.

The Dal Khalsa now carried their arms into the trans-Yamuna territories of Najib ud-Daulah, the *vakil-i-mutliq* (plenipotentiary) of Emperor Shah Alam of Delhi. On 17 April 1765, Sikhs reoccupied Lahore. In 1765, the Durrani came again, but he was obliged to be reconciliatory. The *sardars* spurned his overtures. Najib ud-Daulah, alarmed at the growing influence of the Sikhs, resigned. Emperor Shah Alam opened correspondence with Jassa Singh and other *sardars* with a view to securing his trans-Yamuna territories against their raids. The new Wazir of the emperor, Abdul Ahad Khan, who had led an imperial force against Raja Amar Singh of Patiala in 1779, was beaten back by Jassa Singh. He returned the entire tribute i.e. booty and pillage collected from the Sikhs and paid Rs 7, 00,000 as an indemnity to Dal Khalsa.

As a leader of Dal Khalsa, Jassa Singh was highly revered. He had organized the Sikhs militarily, overthrown Afghan power in northern India and won from the Mughal emperor the right for Sikhs to rule independently over territories they had wrested from the Afghans. Jassa Singh Ahluwalia died on 20 October 1783 at the age of 65 and a *samadh* or cenotaph in his honour stands in the precincts of gurdwara Baba Atal, near the Golden Temple at Amritsar.

[5]**Baba Deep or Dip Singh** (1682-1757), the founder of the Shahid *misl* or principality as well as Damdami Taksal (school of Sikh learning), was born in 1682 and belonged to village Pahuvind, 40 km southwest of Amritsar. He received the vows of the Khalsa at Anandpur where he stayed for some time to study the sacred texts under Bhai Mani Singh. He rejoined Guru Gobind Singh at Talvandi Sabo in 1706 and after the latter's departure for the South, stayed on there to look after the sacred shrine, Damdama Sahib.

Later, with a small group of warriors, he joined Banda Singh Bahadur, but parted ways with him in 1714 along with a breakaway group known as Tatt Khalsa. In 1726, he had four copies of the Guru Granth made from the original one prepared by Bhai Mani Singh. In 1732, he went to the rescue of Sardar Ala Singh of Patalia, who had been besieged in Barnala by Manjh and Bhatti Rajputs in collaboration with the *faujdar* of Jullandhur and the *nawab* of Malerkotla. In 1733, when the governor of Lahore sought peace with the Sikhs offering them a nawabship and a *jagir*, Deep Singh with his *jatha* joined Nawab Kapur Singh and other *sardars* at Amritsar to form a larger joint Sikh force, known as Dal Khalsa. Dal Khalsa was soon split into Buddha (veterans) Dal and Taruna Dal (juvenile) for administrative convenience. Taruna Dal was further split into five *jathas* and in 1748 these *jathas* were designated as *misls* (12 in number). Baba Deep Singh headed the Shahid (Martyr) *misl*. This *misl* had its sphere of influence in the south of River Sutlej and its headquarters at Talwandi Sabo (Damdama Sahib). The tower in which Deep Singh lived still stands next to the Takht Sri Damdama Sahib and is known as Burj Baba Deep Singh Shahid.

During his fourth invasion of India in the winter of 1756-57, Ahmad Shah Abdali annexed the Punjab to his Afghan dominions and appointed his son, Taimur, viceroy at Lahore, with the veteran general, Jahan Khan, as his deputy. In May 1757, Jahan Khan invested Amritsar, razed the Sikh fortress of Ram Rauni and filled up the sacred pool. As soon as the news of the desecration reached Baba Deep Singh, he set out with his *jatha* for the Holy City. On the way many Sikhs joined him, till the numbers swelled to 5,000. The two adversaries clashed at Gohlvar village, 08 km from Tarn Taran on **11 November 1757**. In the fierce action that ensued, Deep Singh suffered a mortal injury to his jugular vein near Ramsar. His head was almost severed from his body. Yet so firm was his resolve to reach the holy precincts that he fought his way through, till he fell dead in the close vicinity of the holy temple. A legend grew that it was Baba Deep Singh's headless body holding his decapitated head on his left hand and wielding his *khanda,* (double-edged sword), with his right hand that had fought on until he had redeemed his pledge to liberate the holy shrine. So potent was the legend that over the years it began to be distorted and magnified, that it became difficult for an interested observer to separate the man from the myth.

It must be emphasised that Baba Deep Singh was an old man of 75 years, but he still led all the rest from the front. In those days, when modern amenities did not exist, extensive walking was an indispensible necessity; agriculture demanded a great degree of physical labour; people were simple and ate wholesome food; in other words survival demanded physical robustness and the times accommodated only the strong and the sturdy. Baba Deep Singh belonged to this stock of people.

Two shrines today commemorate this martyr, one on the circumambulatory terrace of the sarovar (pond) surrounding the Golden Temple where he finally fell and the other, Shahidganj Baba Deep Singh Shahid, near Gurdwara Ramsar, where his body was cremated.

[6]**Gurbakhsh Singh** (1688-1764), also known as Gurbakhsh Singh Nihang or Shahid, hailed from the village Lil, in Amritsar district. He was born on 10 April 1688. In 1693 his family shifted to Anandpur where Gurbakhsh Singh took *pahul* of Khalsa on the historic Baisakhi day of 1699. He completed his religious education under Bhai Mani Singh and later joined the Shahid *misl* of Baba Deep Singh. On the death of Baba Deep Singh in 1757, Gurbakhsh Singh organized his own *jatha* (fighting band). In the battles against the Durrani and the Mughals in the eighteenth century, his *dera* (camp) or small group usually formed the vanguard carrying the banner, and was renowned for its acts of gallantry.

During his seventh invasion, on 01 December 1764, Ahmad Shah Durrani entered the precincts of the partially reconstructed Harimandar (which he had demolished two years earlier), at the head of 30,000 troops. Bhai Gurbakhsh Singh with his suicidal band of thirty (30) pounced on the Afghan king and his hordes. It was an unequal clash – thirty pitted against thirty thousand. All of them including Bhai Gurbakhsh Singh (then 76 years old) fell as martyrs. What is remarkable is the raw courage, dare devilry and fearlessness in the face of fearful odds and evident death. Giving an eye-witness account of the action,

Quazi Nur Muhammad, the chronicler who was in the train of the invader, writes in his *Jangnamah*:

When the King and his army reached the Chakk (Amritsar), they did not see any kafir (infidel) there. But a few men staying in a fortress were bent upon spilling their blood and they sacrificed themselves for their Guru…..They were only thirty in number. They did not have the least fear of death. They engaged the Ghazis and spilled their own blood in the process. Thus all of them were slaughtered and consigned to the seventh [hell].

Bhai Gurbakhsh Singh was cremated behind Takht Akal Bunga. Later, a tomb was built on the site which is now known as Shahid Ganj.

Note – All Sikhs are indeed very proud of Baba Gurbakhsh Singh Nihang or Shahid and his daredevil squad plus the brave, suicidal stance that they put up against heavy odds. Baba Gurbakhsh is respected, admired and venerated by the Sikh masses for his boldness and daring. However it was a foolhardy way of dying and against all military teaching and tactics. Nothing was achieved; precious lives were lost, the temple was blown up and the holy pool desecrated. But then this was the way the fanatical Nihangs functioned; they were heedless people, belonging to the suicidal 'do-or-die' school and known for their reckless and rash daredevilry. They did not believe in living to fight another day.

You don't win a war by dying for your country. You win a war by making the other poor dumb bastard die for his. – General George S. Patton (US army general).

[7]**Mahilpur** today is a big town. It has a grand gurdwara named **Gurdwara Shahidan** to commemorate the battle that was fought here. It also has an old and very famous Khalsa College.

HOW THE SIKHS BECAME MILITANT

The first two hundred years of Sikh history (period of the Gurus) from the time Guru Nanak received the divine vision in 1499, to the time Guru Gobind founded the Khalsa in 1699, can be neatly divided into two equal parts. During the first one hundred years, the first five Gurus preached an egalitarian, monotheistic, non-idolatrous order, free of meaningless form and ritual. The social order was free of caste distinction and the doors of Sikh temples were thrown open to everyone. The Brahmin and the *Shudra* (untouchable) were to break bread together. It was an eclectic, simple and peaceful reformist, movement. No wonder it appealed to one and all (the Hindu and Muslim alike) and moreover it was preached by modest men who laid no claim to kinship with God or garb their utterances as prophecies. They were all holy, peace-loving and humanitarian men.

In 1606 Guru Arjun the fifth Guru was tortured to death. The main reason for this cold blooded murder was the growing popularity of Guru Arjun. Emperor Akbar's death brought a sudden reversal in the policy of the state towards the Sikhs. Religious fanatics like Sheikh Ahmad Sirhindi were able to prevail upon the new Emperor Jahangir and poison his mind against Guru Arjun. The Emperor's son Khuram (Shah Jahan), a religious bigot was the governor of Punjab.

The blessing sought and given by the Guru to Prince Khusro when the latter revolted against his father and happened to be passing that way, came as a ready pretext and an immediate excuse to carry out the execution. The Guru was a religious man and kept an open house. He would have received and blessed anyone even if the visitor had not been of royal blood. Guru Arjun was accused of supporting a rebel and fined heavily. On refusing to pay this fine, he was apprehended and put behind bars. He was subjected to extreme physical torture and on 30 May 1606 he passed away. This was a premeditated move by the Emperor, who was looking for an appropriate occasion to enact the ignoble deed. It was an act of indiscretion on the part of the emperor who should not have treated a holy person like Guru Arjun as an ordinary criminal.

The action was preplanned and predetermined because Jahangir was on the lookout for an opportunity and expressed his desire in his autobiography, the Tzuk-i-Jehangiri thus – "A Hindu named Arjun lived in Goindwal in the garb of a saint. So many of the simple-minded Hindus, nay many foolish Muslims too, had been fascinated by his (Guru's) ways and teaching. He was noised about as a religious and worldly leader. They called him Guru, and from all directions crowds of fools would come to him and express great devotion to him. This busy traffic had carried on for three or four generations. For years the thought had been presenting itself to me that I should either put an end to this false traffic, or he should be brought into the fold of Islam." This action of Jahangir was prompted both by religious feelings and political considerations. Guru Arjun was the first Sikh Guru to fall afoul of the Mughal authorities, thus setting the tone for the remaining history of the Mughal Empire. The martyrdom of Guru Arjun Dev was a turning point in the history of the Sikhs and had far reaching consequences. It altered the course of history. This event, more than any other, converted the Sikh community into a warrior community. The supreme sacrifice of the Guru severed the cordial relations between the Sikhs and Mughals, the Sikh religion became more popular and the Sikhs slowly started following the path of militancy. **Thus were sown the first seeds of that bitter and implacable enmity** that afterwards came to exist between Muslim and Sikh. As Dr Gokul Chand Narang puts it, "His execution was universally regarded by the Hindus as a sacrifice for their faith. The whole of Punjab began to burn with indignation and revenge."

The first five Gurus were peaceful religious and social reformers; the last five had to take steps to carry on this work against increasingly hostile military forces. Seeing the war clouds gathering, during his imprisonment the fifth Guru asked his son Guru Hargobind to sit fully armed on his throne and to maintain an army of saint-soldiers in order to face the approaching storm. The Sikhs started taking steps towards becoming belligerent after the execution of their Guru-Arjun Dev and began to change from a pacifist to a militant people. Guru Hargobind built the Sikh community into a military power. He elevated martyrdom to an ideal of the religion; this was not merely dying for the faith but being killed while fighting for the Sikh community. As instructed by his father, the young Guru Hargobind sat on the *Gurugaddi* fully armed with two swords girded around his waist, on his turban he wore the emblem of royalty and was addressed as *Sacha Badshah* (the true king). One sword symbolized spiritual power and the other temporal (***Miri and Piri***). Henceforth it was a **call to arms**. The Sikhs were asked to bring offerings of arms and horses instead of money. At this point in history, the Sikh community began to actively resist the Mughal Empire and several battles were fought between the two sides. Guru Hargobind had to fight four small battles that were thrust upon him. The remarkable thing about these battles is that the Guru won all of them and all the four enemy commanders were slain by the Guru in duels. The concept of *Miri* and *Piri* by the sixth Guru changed the Sikh Psyche from purely religious to include the military component.

The next major incident that antagonized the Sikhs and made their hackles rise was the most gruesome, cold-blooded murder of their ninth Guru and his three companions. In order to curb the increasing power of the Sikhs the Mughal administration ordered the execution of Guru Tegh Bhahadur. Guru Tegh Bahadur was beheaded on 11 November 1675. Bhai **Mati Das** was sawn alive into two, Bhai **Dayal Das** was boiled alive in boiling water and **Sati Das** was roasted alive wrapped in cotton wool. They died in order to protect the Hindu faith and their refusal to convert to Islam. This was sheer high handedness on the part of Aurangzeb, the Mughal emperor. The times were such; might was right; Islam was considered the only true religion; the Mughal reigned supreme and did what they liked. Aurangzeb had embarked on a most dastardly path of converting the whole of India into Islam. Human rights and dignity did not exist. The Hindu lived in a miserable condition with untold brutalities and many fold atrocities were committed on him.

Martyrdom of the two Sikh Gurus along with their countless devout Sikhs and the general tyranny of the age brought forth a new determination and vigour to the young nation under the tenth Guru. Guru Gobind was a powerful military general with a profound vision of transforming the suppressed and downtrodden people into an aggressive, warlike society – an absolute necessity for a community surrounded by a hostile and powerful empire. It was now left to Guru Gobind Singh to awaken and unite the people divided among themselves on the basis of caste and creed. Since ages foreign invaders had taken advantage of this division amongst the people of Hindustan. One of the biggest lessons that the British learnt after the Mutiny was to keep the caste divisions intact so that they could divide and rule. Guru Gobind Singh was a far sighted man and was looking into the future. It was now for him to arouse and raise the spirits of the meek and timid Hindus and forge a casteless militant fraternity that could fight for its rights. On being confronted by the enemy or when in dire states, these cowardly and frightened folk, refused to fight back, foregoing their identity and begged their oppressors for mercy. This timidity had to be shed and hence forth the tide reversed. "When all other means have failed, it is righteous to draw the sword," Guru Gobind Singh said, "Light your understanding as a lamp and sweep away the filth of timidity." With this mission in mind he earnestly set about to "teach the sparrow how to hunt the hawk and one man to have courage to fight a legion."

It was only after duly considering the given times and conditions, earnestly debating the prevailing situation, profound rumination, and serious deliberation that Guru Gobind decided to form the Khalsa (a brotherhood of saint soldiers) on *Vaisakhi day* the **29 of March 1699** and bless them with the five Ks. He roused the dormant warlike instincts of his followers. By making his followers easily recognizable, by virtue of their beards and turbans, the Guru raised a body of fearless warriors who would not be able to deny their faith when in danger. Their external appearance would invite persecution and in turn make them dauntless and thus breed courage to resist it. It was a movement, a revolution, a storm, a blitzkrieg that swept people off their feet.

The Khalsa was in fact a need of the times – a historical necessity. There is no doubt that the creation of the Khalsa is the single most important event in Sikh history. It was an occurrence of great significance and a major turning point in Sikh history. It fully unified the community and made it a force to reckon with militarily. After the formation of the Khalsa, the political and military power of the Sikhs grew tremendously. It heralded the rising of a great people and created lions out of jackals. It gave birth to Saint Soldiers, there was many fold increase in the number of Sikhs as the down trodden and oppressed sections of society were raised to a high status and given a distinct identity. So there was successful opposition to Mughal rule which finally crumbled and fell. "The object that the Guru (Gobind Singh) set before himself was to infuse a new life in the dead bones of Hindus to make them forget their differences and present a united front against the tyranny and persecution to which they were exported." – G. C. Narang.

By the turn of the sixteenth century more than half of the population of Punjab had already been converted to Islam and there was no check in sight. The march of Islam from Mecca to convert the whole world was stalled in India by the Sikhs and later Ranjit Singh, the Maharaja of the Sikhs, not only stemmed the tide of Islam, but also reversed it. It may not be wrong to say that had the Sikhs not taken up the sword, the whole of north India would be reading the Quran, today.

Born therefore, as a peaceful and tolerant religion, Sikhism was gradually transformed from a purely religious movement, by the persecutions of fanatical bigots like Aurangzeb and the inhuman brutalities of his weak and debauched successors into a military and political movement directed against the weakness and inhumanity of the later Mughal rulers. **The pursuit of arms and devotion to steel was rendered the religious duty of the Sikhs. The Sikhs took to arms in real earnest and thus became militant in the true sense.** There was no looking back now. The Sikhs fought many a battle after this and their fighting qualities and courage and bravery became legendary.

Indeed, the challenge of the Mughal Empire was the turning point in the history of the Sikhs. If the mighty Mughal government had left the Sikhs in peace, free to sing their hymns and to develop their *langars*, it is quite probable that Sikhism would have remained a comparatively obscure provincial cult. Persecution brought it to the stage of Indian history.

Through blood, sweat and tears it walked to political power; the peaceful sect established by Guru Nanak developed into the invincible Khalsa.

– Dr. A. C. Banerjee

As a matter of fact, Sikhism grew out of the necessity of suppressing the oppressors. Thousands of simple peasants flocked to the banner of the Khalsa in order to present a united front to the Moslems and wreak vengeance on them for their barbaric, inhuman and intolerant behavior towards a peace-loving people who were quietly and meekly following their faith. It may be said that had the Moslems been tolerant to the Hindus there would have been no Sikhs.

- Dr. A. C. Banerjee (in his book Anglo-Sikh relations)

RELIGIOUS MOVEMENTS

When the Sikhs attained political power, they deviated from the Sikh values and teachings of their Gurus. Degeneration and decadence had set in. Brahmanical Hinduism came back into its own. The nobility aped the Hindu Rajput princes and followed all their rituals and practices. Besides their unshorn hair, beards and turbans and bowing before the Granth, there was no Sikkhi left in them. The sovereign opulence brought affluence, wealth and luxury, which in turn produced immorality and irreligiousness. At the same time during the Sikh rule, the Hindus of western Punjab and Derajat came under the influence of Sikhism. A few accepted baptisms and joined the Khalsa fraternity; most others continued to describe themselves as Hindus, but read the Granth, went to Gurdwaras and followed all Sikh practices. The cause for this was the appeal of a simple, casteless, egalitarian, monotheistic and non-idolatrous order, free of meaningless form and ritual and the protection (safety and security) provided by the Khalsa in a hostile environment – so they felt that their future lay in mergence with that of the Khalsa. Among these Hindus there grew a custom of bringing up at least one son as a kesadhari (with unshorn hair) Sikh. This was to identify and show solidarity with the Khalsa. This half-Hindu, half-Sikh community belonged to the Khatri, Arora, or Bania castes. They continued to marry within their castes regardless of the change in their religious beliefs.

Three religious movements namely the Nirankari, Namdhari and Radha Soami came into being after the Punjab was annexed by the British. The first two were a result of the changing circumstances and status of the Sikhs – their rise from rural poverty and persecution to sovereignty and opulence; then subjugation by a foreign race and back to penury and oppression. The first stage brought prosperity and prosperity in turn produced wealth, dissipated living and decline in religious values; the second stage, led to anger and nostalgia for the golden age that had passed. The Nirankaris and the Namdharis are an example of these themes. Both of them aimed at maintaining the purity, prestige and splendour of Sikhism and bringing Sikhism back to its pristine glory. Both these sects had taken birth in the north-west – the Nirankaris at Rawalpindi and the Namdharis at Hazro (Attock). The founders of these three sects were greatly influenced by the teachings of Adi Granth and they all owe much to Sikhism – their gurus' discourses are largely drawn from the Adi Granth. The basic differences of these three sects from the main stream or orthodox Sikhism are that they all follow a living guru and have their own separate gurdwaras. The Nirankaris and the Namdharis install the Guru Granth Sahib in their gurdwaras whereas the Radha Soamis do not; they have a raised platform where their guru sits to deliver a discourse. The three sects are strict vegetarians and abstain from tobacco and alcohol. The founders of all the three sects were Hindus, though a Sikh, Balak Singh is accredited for having founded the Namdhari sect, but the inspiration and motivation came from the sermons of one Jawahar Mal a Vaishnavite Hindu whose follower he was. Barring the Namdharis, the other two sects do not believe in the Sikh baptism and the militant vows of the Khalsa, though the gurus of these sects (besides the splinter groups of Agra Radha Soamis) and Sikh followers may be kesadhari. Their form of greeting is also different from the Sikh Sat Sri Akal. Nirankaris use 'dhan nirankar', Radha Soamis 'radha soami' and Namdharis 'sat akal purakh'. Majority of the followers of the Nirankaris and Radha Soamis are mostly Hindus and Sahajdhari Sikhs of the Khatri and Arora trading castes, with a sprinkling of Muslims, Christians and Parsis. The Nirankaris and Radha Soamis emphasize the teachings of Guru Nanak without mentioning the Khalsa of Guru Gobind Singh and differ from main stream Sikhs in their disapproval of the militant brotherhood of the Khalsa, though they may have kesadhari followers. Basically the three sects were reform movements within Sikhism. Today a lot of their ceremonial rites and customs have changed with the times and circumstances and they have their own vested interests and motives.

The Nirankari sect was founded by Dyal Das (d.1855), a bullion merchant of Peshawar. He belonged to this Hindu-Sikh community mentioned above. He condemned idol worship and making obeisance to "holy" men; he disapproved of going on pilgrimages and performing Brahmanical ritual. The positive aspect of his teaching was that God was formless – nirankar (hence the futility of worshipping idols or "saints"). The Narankaris were opposed by the Hindu Brahmins and the Bedi descendants of Guru Nanak and hence ostracised by both Hindus and Sikhs. The chief contribution of the Nirankaris was to standardise ritual connected with births, marriages and deaths based on the Guru Granth (this was done by their second guru Darbara Singh s/o Dyal Das). The Nirankaris claim that they were the first to introduce the Anand marriage (Anand Marriage Act was passed in 1909). The importance of the movement lies largely in the fact that it initiated ceremonial rites which inculcated among the Sikhs a sense of separateness and thus checked the process of their absorption into Hinduism. In 1929 Boota Singh (1883-1944) broke away from the main Nirankari movement and established a separate Sant Nirankari sect and after an altercation/ controversy with the Sikhs, stopped installing the Sri Guru Granth Sahib in the Sant Nirankari gurdwaras. The disintegrated group of Sant Nirankaris has their headquarters at Delhi whereas the original sect has its headquarters at Chandigarh.

The **Radha Soami** sect was founded by a Hindu banker, Shiv Dyal (1818-1878), of Agra. Shiv Dyal was greatly influenced by the teachings of the Adi Granth, and propounded a doctrine which contained elements of both Hinduism and Sikhism. He described God as the union between *radha* (symbolising the soul) and *Soami*, the Master. On his death, the Radha Soamis split in two: the main centre was at Agra; a branch started by a Sikh disciple, Jaimal Singh (1839-1913), was on the bank of river Beas, not far from Amritsar. The Agra Radha Soamis broke up into different factions. Today they have a flourishing industrial estate in a suburb called Dayalbagh. The Agra centre is more of economic than religious importance. The Beas Radha Soamis soon became independent of the Agra centre and had a succession of gurus (all Sikhs) of their own.

The Radha Soamis only accept the teachings of the first five Sikh Gurus contained in the *Adi Granth* and reject the rest. They have no *kirtan* because they believe that music diverts people's minds from the meaning of the hymns to the simple enjoyment of sound. Although the Radha Soamis owe much to Sikhism, it would be wrong to describe them as a sub-sect of Sikhism. The Radha Soamis stand apart as a non-denominational group born of the impact of Sikhism (minus the Khalsa tradition) on Hinduism. The only justification of treating them along with other Sikh religious movements is their close resemblance to the *sahajdharis*. It illustrates the sort of mélange of Hinduism and Sikhism which is gaining currency in the educated circles of both communities. Their faith has considerable attraction for the religiously inclined educated classes, for the Hindu-oriented Sikh, and the Sikh-oriented Hindu. The Radha Soamis claim the adherence of over a million people of different nationalities and denominations (it is impossible to verify the number as they do not form a distinct and separate sect and are not therefore listed in the census).

The Namdhari or Kuka sect was founded by Balak Singh (1797-1862) an Arora of the Batra sub-caste, of village Hazro (Attock) in the northwest frontier region. He was inspired by the sermons of one Jawhar Mal son of Dayal Chand (a Vaishnavite Hindu) of the Kalal caste, who was strongly drawn to the simple tenets of the Sikh faith and started expounding the Granth. Jawhar Mal preached simplicity and disapproved of Brahmanical rituals. He also preached the virtues of poverty and denounced the rich as godless. Balak Singh followed suit by exhorting his followers to live simple lives and practice no religious ritual except repeating Gods name or *nam* (hence *namdhari*). Balak Singh was succeeded by Ram Singh (a carpenter by caste), who has been the greatest guru of the Namdharis. He brought some changes in the forms of worship, dress and address which distinguished the Namdharis from other Sikhs. His disciples chanted hymns and, like dancing dervishes worked themselves into frenzy and emitted loud shrieks or *kuks* (thus the name ***Kukas***).

Most Namdharis come from poorer sections of Sikhs and wear the simplest of clothes that include only white handspun cloth, necklaces of woolen rosaries, carry a stave in their hand, bind their turban flat across their forehead and greet each other with *sat akal purakh*. The Namdharis more strictly adhere to the puritanical faith of Guru Nanak and Guru Gobind than other Sikhs. Their gurdwaras are not ostentatious and they lead simple, thrifty and austere lives. Ram Singh criticised idolatry and caste-ism and also many prevailing malpractices that had crept into Sikhism. Female infanticide, sexism, begging, dowry (giving or taking), tobacco, snuff, alcohol, and meat are strictly forbidden for them. They consider Guru Gobind's *Granth* as the only extant and true sacred writing.

Despite his criticism of many Hindu practices, Ram Singh became an ardent protector of the cow. Cow slaughter had been banned under

Sikh rule, but it was reintroduced by the British. Kuka fanatics murdered some Muslim butchers and their families in Amritsar and then also at Raikot (Ludhiana district). Eight Kukas were hanged and others sentenced to long terms of imprisonment. Kuka passions were inflamed and in January 1872 one gang ignoring their guru's advice decided to attack Malerkotla, a Muslim state where cow slaughter was permitted. On the way to Malerkotla this gang raided the house of a Sikh zamindar (land lord) to acquire arms. L. Cowan the deputy commissioner apprehended 68 of them and after sending a note to the commissioner, T. D. Forsythe, and without any formality blew up 66 of them by tying them to the mouths of cannons. Subsequently another 16 Kukas were blasted off by canons. Whatever sympathy the Sikh may have had for this revivalist movement of the Namdharis turned to anger and indifference for this misguided action of theirs and they became unsympathetic. Baba Ram Singh with 12 of his lieutenants was exiled to Rangoon where he died on 29 November 1884. Of the two English officers L. Cowan was dismissed from service and the commissioner, T. D. Forsythe was transferred outside Punjab.

The Namdharis have a place in the history of the freedom movement of India. Ram Singh was the first man to evolve non-co-operation and the use of *swadeshi* (indigenous goods) as political weapons. In the 1860's Ram Singh advocated the wearing of home spun cloth (*khaddar*), boycott of British goods, government schools, law courts and postal system. This was taken up again by Mahatma Gandhi 60 years later.

CHRISTIAN AND HINDU MISSIONARY ACTIVITY - An American Presbyterian Mission was established at Ludhiana in 1835 and after the annexation of Punjab, Christian missionaries spread their activities into the erstwhile kingdom of Maharaja Ranjit Singh.

Within a short time there was rampant propagation and spread of Christianity. Various Christian orders vied with each other in gaining converts. English officials actively supported the Christian missionaries. The conversions of aristocratic and educated families disturbed the Sikh leaders more than the loss of untouchable Sikhs. Some prominent converts were Maharaja Dalip Singh (1853), Raja Harnam Singh from the royal family of Kapurthla (1847) and Sadhu Sundar Singh a Jat Sikh (1903). The spate of conversions carries on unabated even today.

More serious than the activities of the Christian missions was the challenge of renascent Hinduism especially **Arya Samaj** (discussed later in the chapter). There was also an influx of Bengali intellectuals. The Bengalis preached liberal Hinduism of **Raja Ram Mohan Roy** (1771-1833) and the **Brahmo Samaj** (founded by Raja Ram Mohan Roy and Debendranath Tagore in 1828) and won a notable convert in Dayal Singh Majithia (founder of The Tribune newspaper in 1881 and the Dyal Singh College and public library in Lahore). Raja Ram Mohan Roy was a polyglot and a great religious and social reformer. He preached the unity of God and the brotherhood of man. He was against idol worship, caste system, blind faith, superstition and sacrifices. In the social field he worked for (i) eradication of *Sati* and female infanticide (ii) widow remarriage (iii) abolishing polygamy and empowerment of women (iv) promotion of education and (v) improving the lot of peasants.

Swami Vivekananda (original name Narendra Datta – born Jan. 12, 1863, Calcutta – died July 4, 1902, Calcutta) a Hindu spiritual leader and reformer, also later joined the Brahmo Samaj and became the most notable disciple of RAMAKRISHNA and went on to found the Ramakrishna Mission. There were lot of similarities between the teachings of Sikhism and Brahmo Samaj. Many *Brahmo Mandirs* and

Shantiniketan recite from the Sikh scriptures and Brahmo Samaj Sangeet i.e. their hymns include many shabads of Guru Nanak. Guru Nanak Dev *ji's* birthday is celebrated even now in Shantiniketan with *Deepmala* and *Aarti* in Bengali. There is a lot of Sikh literature written by Bengali authors in Bengali and English. Many works including the Guru Granth have been translated into Bengali. The father and son duo of Maharishi Debendranath and Rabindranath Tagore (Nobel Laureate), who were followers of Brahmo Samaj were greatly influenced by Sikhism. They visited Amritsar and the Golden Temple a number of times. Rabindranath Tagore had a life long association with Sikhism and its history as depicted in his writings and poems on Sikh themes. Another society known as the **Sat Sabha** was founded by some Bengali and Punjabi Hindu gentlemen.

The **Theosophical Society** founded by Dr. Anne Besant (1847-1933) also had an impact and influence in Punjab. Theosophy is a philosophy which believes that knowledge of God may be achieved through such things as intuition, meditation, and prayer. Anne Besant became an Indian independence leader and established the Indian Home rule League in 1916.

Interest in India and the Hindu religion was generated by the publication of a plethora of literature by English authors. This was followed by many works on Punjab. What Monier Williams did for India, Dr G. W. Leitner sought to do for Punjab. A German Dr Ernest Trumpp (1828-85) an eminent linguist translated into English portions of the Guru Granth in his book titled 'The Adi Granth' (first published in 1877). But his approach was prejudiced and his conclusions were not only offensive, they were insulting as well. This wrong was set right in 1909 by a wonderful man named Max Arthur Macauliffe. After leaving a lucrative job, toiling for over 20 years and spending a large amount of money Macauliffe wrote the book '*The Sikh Religion*' in six volumes. This book is popular to this day and is being printed and exported to western countries for large Sikh populations there. Macauliffe introduced *Sikhi* to the English speaking west. He converted to Sikhism in the 1860s and was derided by his British employers for having "turned a Sikh." His personal assistant remarked in his memoirs that on his death bed, Macauliffe could be heard reciting the Sikh morning prayer, **Japji Sahib**, ten minutes before he died.

THE ARYA SAMAJ was founded in 1875, by Swami Dayanand Saraswati (1824-1883), an ascetic and a religious and social reformer. Dayanand was born 1824, Tankara (Gujarat) and died October 30, 1883, Ajmer (Rajasthan). His original name was Mula Sankara. He was a zealot, Saivite Gujarati Brahmin of Kathiawar. **He rejected what he considered idol worship** at 14 after seeing mice swarm over an image of Shiva, attracted by offerings placed before it. He was profoundly moved by this incident which left a deep imprint on his psyche and radically changed his thinking. In 1863, Dayanand began preaching his vision of reinstating a purified Vedic religion. His motto was "back to Vedas." Dayanand was a forceful orator and within a few years his voice was heard all over India.

The two Swamis, Dayanand and Vivekananda, were both against idol worship. Dayanand's iconoclastic casteless egalitarianism, monotheism and non-idolatrous beliefs had a special appeal for the Sikhs. So when he came to Punjab in the summer of 1877, he received a grand welcome from the Sikhs and Hindus. He opened a branch of the Arya Samaj at Lahore.

Proselytisation (*sudhi*-purification) was an important part of the Arya Samaj's activities, and it gained many Hindu and Sikh adherents; prominent ones among them being Lala Lajpat Rai (born in a Hindu-

Sikh family), Ajit Singh (paternal uncle of Sardar Bhagat Singh) and Hans Raj. The Arya Samaj expanded rapidly, but their hate mongering, bigotry, communalism, rabid fanaticism and rigidity did not take them long to become anti-Sikh. To Dayanand the Granth of the Sikhs was a book of secondary importance; Sikh gurus men of little learning and the Sikh theologians contemptuous people because of their ignorance of Sanskrit (a language which was not vernacular and the common people did not speak or understand it); moreover the pundits considered it *deva bhasa* (language of the gods and taboo/forbidden to Sudras, i.e. members of low castes). The infallibility of the Vedas (which sanctioned 'caste system' was against the very basic Sikh tenets) was uncompromising to Dayanand and his followers.

The Sikh religion has no priestly order and no sacraments and denounces priest craft, hypocrisy and idolatry; it preaches simplicity, egalitarianism, democracy, liberalism and secularism; hence it could not have a caste-ridden society, a language not understood or spoken by the people and a religion full of rituals, dominated and monopolized by a priestly class. Sikhism was trying to free people from the clutches of greedy and capricious Brahmins; all learning was in the hands of the priesthood, and this led to serious abuses.

The Arya Samajists not only insulted and abused the Sikh Gurus but also ridiculed the community by publicly shaving a number of Sikhs at Lahore and other places. It was all the more painful for the Sikhs as it was they who had first invited Dayanand to Punjab, arranged his lectures at Jullundur, Amritsar, etc. and had protected him against the Sanatan Dharmi Hindus and also the Muslims and Christians on whom he poured abuse in his writings and speeches.

As mentioned earlier, the Brahmo Samaj had won a notable convert in **Dyal Singh Majithia**. Like Pandit Shiv Narayan Agnihotri (1850-1929), the founder of **Dev Samaj** (a religious and social reform society, akin to Brahmo Samaj), Dyal Singh Majithia, had earlier (before joining Brahmo Samaj), discussed the tenets of the Arya Samaj with its founder Swami Dayanand. Then after investigating and examining (vetting/perusing) the canons, he had rejected them and refused to side with any faction of the Arya Samaj. Pandit Agnihotri even went to the extent of defending Brahmo ideals in opposition to the new Arya Samaj and he also defended Sikhism against attacks made by Arya Samaj in 1888-89. The second major leader of the **Sat sabha** Pandit Bhanu Datta Basant Ram, the Acharya of the society, played a prominent role in the religious debates among Punjabi Hindus and even opposed the Arya Samaj when Swami Dayanand came to Lahore in 1877.

Through the efforts of the Singh Sabha, the Sikhs were now better aware of their religion and its true and glorious past. Dayanand was an outsider (Gujarati) and did not understand the Punjabi psyche. The Sikhs rejected the Vedas and Sanskrit and turned their backs on Dayanand because of his rigidity, rabid bigotry, fundamentalism, and anti-Sikh bias; instead they joined the Muslims and Christians in fiercely resisting the Arya Samaj. The Singh Sabha retaliated by carrying proselytising activities into the Arya Samaj camp and the more the Samajists claimed **Sikhism to be a branch of Hinduism**, the more the Sikhs insisted that they were a distinct and separate community. This action and reaction had a decisive bearing on the course of Hindu-Sikh relations and broke up the close social relationship which had existed between the two sister communities. It found expression in the publication of a booklet *Ham Hindu Nahin Hain* (*We are not Hindus*) by the scholarly Kahan Singh, who was then chief minister of Nabha. This opposition and animosity between the two communities is discernible even today.

Dera Sacha Sauda is a sect of comparatively recent origin. It was founded in Baluchistan by a Sikh Baba, Beparvah Mastana on 29 April 1948. The name suggests him to be a follower of Sufi thought or persuasion. Shah Satnam Singh was the next spiritual leader and Gurmeet Ram Rahim Singh (born 15 August 1967), who took over on 23 September 1990 is the present head of the Dera. The sect uses the basis of Sikhism and has borrowed heavily from the Sikh religion, using quotes from *Gurbani* to gain support among the popular mass of the public. According to the Dera, all religions are equally honoured and welcomed; the Dera claims to believe in humanity as the greatest religion and accordingly professes to be involved in the service of man-kind. The poor, helpless and sick are helped here in every possible manner. The Dera's appeal is mainly to the marginalized and backward (uneducated) sections of the *Dalits* -- a potent political force which the Dera chief successfully uses as a vote bank. It is a mouth piece for the Dalits. The organisation affirms to be a non-profit, social welfare and spiritual organization working on the guiding principles of secularism, equality, non acceptance of materialistic wealth, meditation, truth and faith over everything else. It also has a welfare and disaster relief organization. On 28 August 2017, the self-styled god man, Gurmeet Ram Rahim Singh was convicted in rape cases and is undergoing imprisonment for 20 years. There are a number of rape, murder and misappropriation of funds (donated by his followers for a noble cause) cases against him.

THE SINGH SABHA AND SOCIAL REFORM (SIKH RENAISSANCE) MOVEMENT

The inherent weakness of the Sikh body politic, the activities of Christian missions, the proselytisation by a new Hindu organisation called Arya Samaj and the rationalism that came with the introduction of scientific concepts were some of the factors that led to the disintegration of the Sikh people. The decline in moral standards resulted in decadence as evils and malpractices in society thrived unabated. Real (orthodox) Sikhs decreased in numbers. In fact Sikhism itself was on the wane.

The Singh Sabha Movement was a reformist movement among the Sikhs in the 70s of the nineteenth century following closely on the heels of the three successive religious movements, the Nirankari, Namdhari and Radha Soami. It became a vital rejuvenating force at a time when Sikhism was fast losing its distinctive identity. It was quite different from its precursor movements in source, content and outcome. The earlier religious movements came into being for the revival of puritan Sikhism. Unhappy at the dilution of Sikh doctrine and practice, they desired to create an awakening and set right some of the aberrations purely religious in nature. All three earlier religious movements (Nirankari, Namdhari and Radha Soami) ultimately developed into schismatic coteries with their own gurus and esoteric ritual. In contrast the Singh Sabha movement arose out of a common awareness of the danger to the very existence of the Sikhs as a separate religious community. It was led by men deeply religious but with no claims to divine knowledge and no ambitions for exalted priesthood. As it had a strong and rational basis, it possessed a mass appeal. It influenced the entire community and reoriented its outlook and spirit. In fact it stimulated and has shaped the Sikhs' attitude and aspirations for nearly a century and a half now.

Some intellectual Sikhs who were perturbed by the rapid depletion in their numbers, general laxity in religious observances among themselves and other happenings around them, convened a meeting at Amritsar on 30 July 1873; it was decided to form an association which should adopt measures to defend the Sikh faith against the onslaught of Christian missionaries as well as others. The name proposed for the body was Sri Guru Singh Sabha. Its first formal meeting took place in front of the Akal Takht on 01 October 1873. The main objectives of the Singh Sabha were (i) to propagate the true Sikh religion and restore Sikhism to its pristine glory; (ii) to edit, publish and circulate historical and religious books; (iii) to propagate current knowledge using Punjabi as the medium and to start magazines and newspapers in Punjabi; (iv) to reform and bring back the apostates into the Sikh fold; and (v) draw attention of the high placed Englishmen to social and religious reforms of the Sikhs and also to ensure their association with the education programme of the Sabha. It was the Singh Sabha's policy to avoid criticism of other religions and discussion of political matters.

Under the prevailing circumstances, the Sikhs had no option but to seek guidance from their rulers. They needed the help and patronage of the government. In order to ensure this they resolved to cultivate loyalty to the crown and under the auspices of the Singh Sabha, the Sikhs sought and won the collaboration of English officials in their drive for literacy. British officers headed management committees, appointed key officials, and in general provided grants and facilities to ensure continued Sikh sympathy for the raj. Another Singh Sabha was set up at Lahore on 02 November 1879. The movement picked up momentum and many Singh Sabhas appeared at many places not only in Punjab but also in several parts of India and abroad from London in the west to Shanghai (China) in the east. Singh Sabha General (renamed **Khasa Diwan** soon after) was set up on 11 April 1880 as a coordinating body at Amritsar. But soon ideological differences among the office bearers led to another Khalsa Diwan being set up at Lahore. Despite the mutual bickering and even litigation, both the Diwans worked for the same aims with the same programmes. The Lahore Diwan was more dynamic; had more number of Singh Sabhas under it and comprised of enlightened and educated men who were freeing themselves from the thralldom of priesthood by seeking to purge their religion of all the grossness that had clung to it by the devices of the priestly class.

The Amritsar Diwan was conservative and considered Sikhs as a part of the Hindu community and Sikhism as an offshoot of Hinduism; they claimed special position, privileges and reverence for the priestly class and the descendants of the Gurus (Bedis and Sodhis); they wanted curbs on the untouchable Sikhs to worship in the gurdwaras and they wanted that Khalsa College be established at Amritsar. **The Lahore Diwan** wanted progressive reforms and believed Sikhism to be a separate sovereign religion having equality of all believers without distinction of caste or status as its basic creed. They were in favour of severing all ties with old established social customs and practices and they wanted the Khalsa College established at Lahore. Ultimately the two Diwans patched up their differences and the outcome was the formation at Amritsar on 30 October 1902 of the **Chief Khalsa Diwan** pledged to "cultivate loyalty to the crown," safeguard Sikh rights vis-à-vis the other communities, and to fight for adequate representation of Sikhs in services, particularly the army. Almost from its inception the most effective leader was Sunder Singh Majithia (1872-1941).

The most important aspects of Singh Sabha movement were educational and literary. The foundation of the Khalsa College was laid on 05 March 1892 at Amritsar. Orphanages, a system of Sikh schools, institutions for training preachers and *granthis* (readers of the Guru Granth) were built. One of the best known institutions was the Sikh Kanya Maha Vidyalaya of Ferozepur. The teaching of Gurmukhi and Sikh scriptures was compulsory in these Khalsa schools. The impetus given to education in its turn stimulated the publication of books, magazines, tracts, and newspapers. Another milestone was the establishment of the Sikh Educational Conference convened annually since its inception in 1908 to the present day. The goal was to take stock of the progress of literacy in the community, collect money to strengthen and improve the project and add to the number of existing schools. Other achievements of the Diwan were the removal of idols from the compound of the Darbar Sahib, Amritsar (1905), passing of the Anand Marriage Act 1909, and the preparation of a common code of conduct for the Sikhs, giving in detail the way they should perform their ceremonies (1916).

Although the Singh Sabha movement had done a remarkable job in the field of education and to revitalize the religious spirit of the Sikhs, it failed to cleanse the rot that had set in the Sikh religious places under the management of a corrupt and degenerate priesthood that was secure under legal protection. Loyalty to the government in order to seek favours for the community was one of the bases of the strategy of the Divan, but the political climate in the country had started changing with the advent of the freedom struggle. The Chief Khalsa Divan continued to pursue a soft stance and the path of helpless inactivity for fear of British displeasure. From 1914 onwards the movement began to lose its popularity and hold on the Sikh masses. On 13 April 1919, occurred the Jallianwala Bagh massacre which radically changed the political as well as religious scenario in which the Chief Khalsa Diwan became practically irrelevant, and the central stage was occupied by the **Gurdwara Reform movement**. Notwithstanding the fact that the Singh Sabha movement petered out in the 1920's it left a legacy of a chronically defensive attitude towards Hinduism.

The Chief Khalsa Divan is active till date, especially in the field of education, and enjoys the affiliation of a large number of local Singh Sabhas. The Singh Sabha movement checked the relapse of the Sikhs into Hinduism. Large numbers of Hindus of northern and western Punjab and Sind became *sahajdhari* Sikhs and the *sahajdharis* were encouraged to become the Khalsa.

THE GURDWARA REFORM MOVEMENT
(1920-1925)

Simplicity is the hallmark of the Sikh faith. The Sikh religion has no priestly order and the only item installed or housed in their gurdwaras is the Guru Granth Sahib. Any person (man or woman) conversant with the Sikh scriptures can read the Granth, worship, pray or preach.

The beginning of religious centres known as *dharamsalas* (later named gurdwaras), all over the country, goes back to the time of Guru Nanak, who had travelled extensively preaching his message. Since he alone could not cater to the needs of thousands of devotees, the third guru, Guru Amar Das (1479-1579) had established 22 *manjis* or *parchar kendras* (parishes) all over India. The fifth guru, Guru Arjun further consolidated the system by appointing accomplished agents (*masands*), to organize, worship and collect offerings. The *masands* were invested with greater authority and more varied religious and social functions. The job of the *masands* (vicar or parish leader) was to preach the faith and collect tithes and offerings from followers in their area or parish and visit the guru at least once in a year with the offerings and batches of Sikhs. *Masands* were chosen for their piety and devotion. The *masand* structure helped in the expansion of the Sikh faith and in knitting together centres established in far flung areas. But as time passed, the *masands* became neglectful of their religious office and took to personal aggrandizement. The last guru, Guru Gobind Singh had to charge them with corruption and oppression and before forming the Khalsa, he abolished the institution of *masands*.

After the abolition of the order of the *masands* (agents) by Guru Gobind Singh and during the troubled years of the eighteenth century when Sikhs suffered severe persecution, they were either busy fighting the Mughals and Pathans or on the run. Throughout the course of this period, the Sikhs were gentlemen at large, because they were being hunted and a price lay on their heads. They had no time to manage their affairs. The **Udasi** *sadhus* (those who renounce the world) and **Mahants** took charge of their places of worship and the preaching of Guru Nanak's word. The job of *granthi* (scripture reader) in those turbulent times was a hazardous one, and many important shrines were entrusted to members of the *Udasi* order, who did not fully subscribe to the Khalsa creed and, being usually clean-shaven, could disclaim their association with Sikhism when their lives were in danger.

The word *Udasi* is derived from the Sanskrit word *udasin*, i.e. one who is indifferent to or disregardful of worldly attachments, a stoic or a mendicant. *Udasi* is an ascetical sect founded by Sri Chand (1494-1629), the elder son of Guru Nanak. Baba Sri Chand lived for well over a century; he travelled the length and breadth of India with his disciples and had many followers. He knew Sanskrit and studied many Sanskrit texts, lived the life of an ascetic, practicing austerities and yoga. **The *Udasis* do not subscribe to Sikh rites and their religious practices are different from the Sikhs. They however read Guru Granth Sahib in their monasteries and revere Guru Nanak like other Sikhs.** The *Udasis* have their own *deras* (a word of Persian extraction, that has several connotations, but is generality used to mean abode or permanent living place) and monasteries all over the country. A *Mahant* belonged to the *Udasi* sect *and* was the superior or principal priest of an *Udasi math* or *akhara* (a word derived from Sanskrit *akspala* or *akswala* meaning stage or theatre or arena, is in common use a sectarian monastery, seminary or seat of Hindu anchorites such as *Saannyasis* and *Bairagis* and Sikh ascetics, *Udasis*, Jagiasi[1] and *Nirmalas*[2]). This term acquired a distinct Sikh application during the eighteenth and nineteenth century period, when many Sikh gurdwaras passed into the hands of hereditary custodians. These men, who became virtual owners of their gurdwaras, were known as *Mahants* and most of them were not initiated Sikhs. The words *dera, math, akhara,* monastery and seminary are more or less synonymous with each other and so are the words *Udasi* and *Mahant* in our context.

During the *misl* (Sikh confederation) period and when the Sikhs acquired power and sovereignty, the bigger gurdwaras received large sums in offerings and the income of some of them ran into several lacs per year. During Sikh rule, most of the historical *gurdwaras* were endowed by Maharaja Ranjit Singh, the Sikh chiefs and nobility with liberal grants of land. The income derived from *jagirs* attached to the shrines also assumed princely proportions. The capital donated and the produce and proceeds from the estates were meant for Guru Ka Langar and the boarding and lodging of pilgrims and travellers. This well-intentioned philanthropy, however, in many cases led to the rise of hereditary priesthood. Even during Sikh rule, the Sikh shrines continued to be looked after by *Udasis*, and the post of *granthi*-cum-manager passed from father to son. It was only the less important gurdwaras that were looked after by honest and humble men who dedicated their lives to prayer and service (*sewa*). With the establishment of British rule, the lands and properties attached to many of the gurdwaras were entered against the names of the *Mahants*.

Since the *Mahants* were recorded as owners, they began to utilize the land and property for their own private purposes, as they wished. A short time after the Jallianwala massacre, Brigadier-General Dyer was honoured by the priests of Darbar Sahib (Golden Temple), Amritsar. The *Udasis* or *Mahants*, who were as much Hindu as they were Sikh, installed idols in the gurdwara to attract Hindu worshippers. As more money flowed into the coffers of the *Mahants*, they became more and more depraved and led easy and immoral lives; there were cases of misuse of gurdwara funds and desecration of the sacred premises. Throughout Sikh rule, the Khalsa wore their hair and beards unshorn and paid obeisance to the Guru Granth. For the rest, they observed all social evils (child marriage, *sati* and female infanticide) and customs and practices, including those strictly forbidden by their Gurus like rituals, caste system, blind faith, superstition, sacrifices etc. There were no rules framed for the management of the gurdwaras and the qualifications required for the priests.

It was the Singh Sabha that brought in education and made the Sikhs aware of their religion and rights. They were the first to protest against the prevention of Sikhs of untouchable castes from entering gurdwaras and the performance of idol worship in some bigger gurdwaras. But the leaders of Singh Sabha were loyalists and believed in following constitutional and ethical procedures for any problem. They made representations to officials and knocked the doors of courts by filing law suits. The government invariably had ulterior motives and stood for vested interests. The official attitude was that a person in whose name a piece of land or property was registered was *prima facie* the owner and could be ousted only by means of a law suit for possession in the civil court. It did not occur to them that the *mahant* of a gurdwara was only a custodian and exactly in the same position as the vicar of a church, in whom no property rights are vested. The legal process was dilatory and prolonged and the costs prohibitive.

The misuse of gurdwara property required more drastic action. Men of nationalist views broke the monopoly of the Singh Sabha over Sikh affairs and set up the Central Sikh League at Amritsar by the end of

1919. A committee known as the *Shiromani Gurdwara Prabandhak Committee* (Central Gurdwara Management Committee - S.G.P.C.) for the management of all Sikh shrines was set up on 15 November 1920. An organisation called Akalis (Immortals) was also formed. Their task was to raise and train men for taking over the gurdwaras from reluctant *mahants*, through peaceful means of non-cooperation and non-violence (later this organisation became a political party–the Akali Dal). Before leaving each *jatha* (band or troop) took a pledge to remain non-violent in word and deed. They were to remain unarmed, silent and peaceful and the only weapon they had was prayer on their lips. This action brought them into conflict with Punjabi Hindus, many of whom unwittingly sided with the *mahants* and the British administration.

Under pressure, which was often followed by show of strength, the mahants began to buckle and hand over control of gurdwaras to elected committees and in some places agreed to become paid *granthis*. However in certain locations, there was violence against the Akalis. This was the background of the Gurdwara Reform Movement.

A letter written by Mr. King, the Commissioner of Lahore Division, assuring the *mahants* of their legal rights, was responsible for some of the resistance and violence by the *mahants*. At **Tarn Taran** Akali volunteers were attacked and two of them were killed. The bloodiest incident took place at **Nankana Sahib** (birthplace of Guru Nanak), on 20 Feb. 1921, where Mahant Narain Das was indulging in immoral practices. He had asked for police protection and hired 400 hoodlums to defend and safeguard his interests. 130 unarmed and non-violent Akalis were butchered in cold blood. The dead and dying were then placed on a pile of logs and burnt. The news of the outrage spread like wild fire and *jathas* (bands or troops) of Akalis began to converge at Nankana. The commissioner of Lahore reached the site and with great alacrity handed over the keys of the shrine to a representative of the S.G.P.C. For this crime, three men were sentenced to death and two, including Narain Das, sentenced to transportation for life.

Amritsar (The Keys Affair) - The attitude of the government became more antagonistic and they used bullying tactics to intimidate the Sikhs. In November 1921, the deputy commissioner of Amritsar took the keys of the treasury of the Golden Temple and contrived to hand them over to his own protégé. Failing to find anyone to become a manager on behalf of the government or to set up a rival committee, the government realised that he had disturbed a hornet's nest and was now about to light an already smoldering fire. The lieutenant governor of Punjab, Sir Edward Maclagan ordered the unconditional release of all Akali prisoners and return of the keys to Kharak Singh's (new president of S.G.P.C.) committee on 17 January 1922. Mahatama Gandhi congratulated the S.G.P.C. through a telegram saying, "first decisive battle of India's freedom won. Congratulations".

After Nankana, the next place where violence against the peaceful Akalis took place was **Guru Ka Bagh**. Every day a *jatha* of a 100 Akalis, wearing black turbans, would take an oath of non-violence at the Akal Takht and then march towards Guru Ka Bagh, chanting sacred hymns. The police stopped them at various points far removed from the site of dispute, beat them mercilessly till they dropped unconscious to the ground. They were then thrown in muddy ditches, to be picked up by medical relief parties. This continued for nineteen days, political leaders, social workers and reporters who came to witness the gruesome scene of the non-violent protest were shocked and the reports of these eye-witnesses stirred the conscience of the world. A.L. Verges, an American cinematographer, made a film of the appalling happenings, under the caption, 'Exclusive Picture of India's Martyrdom'. When Rev. C.F. Andrews (1871-1940), an English missionary and educationist visited the place, he was deeply moved by the noble "Christ-like" behaviour of the Akalis. He sent a detailed first hand report of the brutality and atrocities of the police to the Press, on what he witnessed on 12 September 1922 and also apprised the lieutenant governor. Sir Edward Maclagan arrived at Guru Ka Bagh on 13 September 1922 and ordered an end to the beatings. In the agitation 5,605 Akalis had been arrested and 936 were hospitalised. The Akalis took possession of Guru Ka Bagh and the disputed land.

Jaito *Morcha* was a partially religious agitation. The Akalis launched the Jaito *morcha* (battle-front) on 14 September 1923 in order to assert their religious rights. Passive s*ahidi jathas* were sent to Jaito every day and many Akali leaders were arrested. Gradually the *Jathas* increased in strength from 25 to 100 and then from 100 to 500. While the Jaito *morcha* was still going on the *mahant* at Bhai Pheru in Lahore resiled from his promise to the Akalis and charged them for trespass. In this way a second front was opened and batches of 25 Akalis started going every day to Bhai Pheru. The Indian National Congress declared full sympathy with the *morcha*; among those arrested at Jaito was Jawharlal Nehru.

On 21 February 1924 a passive *jatha* of 500 was mercilessly fired upon by the State forces, on its arrival at Jaito causing some 300 casualties including about 100 killed. Eye-witnesses saw the non-violent and passive members of the *jatha* rushing forward to seek martyrdom when they saw their comrades' fall dead or wounded. Many more *jathas* followed suit to both places but they were all arrested without being fired upon. The unending streams of *jathas* to Jaito and Bhai Pheru exasperated the authorities. The struggle dragged on up to 21 July 1925 when the restrictions on Akhand Path were removed and the Sikhs were allowed to perform the ceremony uninterrupted.

Sikh Gurdwara Act 1925

For quite some time negotiations had been going on for a permanent solution to the Gurdwara problem. The Sikh Gurdwara Act 1925 was passed on 07 July 1925 in the Punjab Legislative Council and it came into force on 01 November 1925. It placed the control of all historical Gurdwaras in the hands of an elected Board which was named the Shromani Gurdwara Prabandhak Commette (S.G.P.C.). This brought to an end the long drawn struggle between the Sikhs and the government on this issue. This legislative Act was ushered in after making innumerable and unprecedented sacrifices during the historical Gurdwara Reform Movement and after liberating Sikh shrines from the hereditary, corrupt, degenerated and deeply entrenched priests called *Mahants*.

The Gurdwara Reform Movement created political awakening in the princely states. After the conflict between the Sikhs and the British government over the gurdwaras had been settled, an agitation started in the states. The Akalis in the states began to raise their voice against the autocratic misuse of power by the maharajas.

Nearly a hundred years have passed since the Sikh Gurdwara Act 1925 was passed on 07 July 1925 and a lot of contribution has been made by the S.G.P.C. to the Sikh religious, educational, social and cultural institutions. However on the negative side all the evils existing in the modern Indian political, democratic system have crept in. The system is completely in the hands of the Sikh political party (the Akali Dal) which determines and monitors all its activities. Rather than the spiritual (*piri*) controlling and guiding the political (*miri*), it is vice versa. As a result the gurdwara management at present is neither fully democratic nor fully corporate. It has been left with no independence or autonomy of its own. It is high time the

Sikhs distinguish between the political management and governance of a state and management of religious shrines. The former has to be segregated from the latter. When the ibid bill was being passed, two pragmatic gentlemen with vision had warned the Sikhs of what was in store for them. These two gentlemen were a Muslim, Sir Fazal-i-Hussain and a British Christian, Lord Malcolm Hailley, the then Governor of Punjab and Chairman of Punjab legislative Assembly. Their predictions are proving true today.

1. **Jagiasi**, also Jagiasu or Jijnasu is a religious sect cognate with the *Udasi* section of the Nanakpanthis of Sindh. The word *jagiasa* is derived from Sanskrit *jijnasa* (desire to know), *jagiasi* denoting one desirous of knowledge, of spiritual insight. The members of the sect are mostly *sahajdharis* i.e. gradualists, believing in the Gurus and following generally the Sikh tenets but not yet sworn as full members of the community. There are however some who accept the rights of Khalsa initiation and wear long hair while some others add the suffix 'Singh' to their names. Following the example of the founder of the sect, Baba Sri Chand, the elder son of Guru Nanak, the Udiasis do not marry. The Jagiasis on the other hand follow the example of the younger son of Guru Nanak, Lakhmi Chand, who was a householder, and take to family life. The sect flourished especially during the days of Baba Gurupat, known to be a descendant of Guru Nanak. He visited Sindh during Sikh times with a letter from Maharaja Ranjit Singh to the local chief, Mir Sohrab Khan. Baba Gurupat established many *Jagiasi tikanas* or seats in Sindh, including those at Khairpur, Hyderabad, Halani, and Kandyaro. His last will, dated 29 July 1857, bears the signatures of many a Sindhi Jagiasi and Udasi saints.

The Jagiasis recite hymns from the Guru Granth Sahib which they venerate as much as any devout Sikh and, like Sikhs, reject idolatry. But they perform several Hindu rituals as well as they do not undergo Sikh baptismal ceremony.

2. **Nirmalas**, derived from the Sanskrit *nirmala* meaning spotless, unsullied, pure, bright, etc. is the name of a sect of Sikhs engaged in religious study and preaching. The sect came into being during the time of Guru Gobind Singh (1666-1708), though some, on the authority of a line in the first *var* of Bhai Gurdas (d. 1636), claim like the Udasis, Guru Nanak (1469-1539) himself to be the founder. Guru Gobind wanted his followers not only to acquire skills in warfare but also to cultivate letters. Guru Gobind once asked one of the scholars employed by him, Pandit Raghunath, to teach Sanskrit to the Sikhs. He refused, saying that Sanskrit was *deva bhasa* (language of the gods) and could not be taught to *Sudras* (low castes). The Guru sent five of his Sikhs, namely Karam Singh, Vir Singh, Ganda Singh, Saina Singh and Ram Singh, dressed as upper-class students, to Varanasi, the centre of Hindu learning. These Sikhs worked diligently for several years and returned to Anandpur as accomplished scholars of classical Indian theology and philosophy. In view of their piety and sophisticated manner, they and their students came to be known as Nirmalas, and were later recognised as a separate sect. The sect has several sub-sects each with its own *dera* (camp/habitation) and following.

The Nirmalas believe in the ten Gurus and Guru Granth Sahib. They generally do not take the Khalsa baptism, don ochre coloured garments, mostly practice celibacy and are devoted to scriptural and philosophical studies. By tradition they are inclined towards classical Hindu philosophy especially Vedanta. They have mastery over the Sanskrit language and the Vedas. Their contribution towards the preaching of Sikh doctrine and production of philosophical literature in Sanskrit, *Braj*, Hindi and Punjabi is considerable. All sacred Hindu texts and a number of other Hindu classics have been translated and a vast number of books in various languages have also been written by them. The headquarters of the Nirmala sect is in Kankhal. They have *Akharas* (monastery/seminary) in all major Hindu centres – Kankhal, Haridwar, Rishikesh, Varanasi (Kashi), Allahabad (Prayag), Ujjain, Gaya, Triyambak (Nasik), Patna, Kurukshetra and also in Punjab.

Now famous as the *Eco Baba,* **Baba Balbir Singh Seechewal** (born 2 February 1962) is a Nirmala Sikh. He single handedly cleaned and restored Kali Bein River, a 160 km long tributary of Beas in Doaba region of Punjab. He says, "It is said in the *Bani* (Guru's gospel) that it is better to save a creature, than to take bath in 68 holy places of pilgrimage". He has been awarded with the Padmashri by the Government of India (2017) and Hero of Environment by TIME MAGAZINE.

SIKH RELIGIOUS BELIEFS

1. Sikhism believes in Oneness of God and Universal Brotherhood of man.

2. Sikhism believes in samsara (reincarnation) and karma (the sum of a person's actions in this and previous lives, seen as affecting their future fate).

   Words do not the saint or sinner make
   Action alone is written in the book of fate. – Guru Nanak

   Truth above all,
   Above truth, truthful conduct. (Nanak)

3. Sikhism is an egalitarian, democratic and secular religion. It recognizes no distinction between man and man and does not believe in the caste system.

   Manas ki jaat sab ek hi pachanbo
   (Know all mankind as one caste) – Guru Gobind Singh

4. Sikhism is one of the most deeply spiritual and profoundly mystical religions of the world, advocating social harmony and egalitarianism unrivalled by any other major religion, with the possible exception of Buddhism.

5. Sikhism believes in **equality of men and women in all respects**. In the Sikh religion women are accorded a very high status. *Purdah* (veil), *sati* (concremation), immurement (imprisonment), female infanticide, dowry, polygamy and child marriage are

strictly forbidden. Female education is encouraged and remarriage of women is allowed. It is the only religion which says in their religious scriptures that women are equal to men in every respect.

From woman is our birth.
In woman's womb are we conceived.
To woman are we wedded.
The woman is our friend.
From woman is the family.
Through woman are our bonds with the world.
Why call woman evil who gives birth to kings and all?
From the woman is the woman, without the woman
There is none. Save the one God alone. – Guru Nanak

6. Sikhs believe in giving a tithe (one-tenth) of earnings in charity.

7. The essence of Sikhism is ***Kirat Karna, Naam Japna, te Vand Chakna*** (Work, Worship and Charity).

8. Sikhism does not believe in asceticism, renunciation, austerity, penances, mortification, celibacy, priest craft, idolatry, ritual, superstition, dogma, caste system, religious intolerance and prejudice against women. A man should not renounce the world, but live the life of a house-holder and a family man and abide pure amid the impurities of the world.

The lotus in the water is not wet
Nor the water-fowl in the stream.
If man would live, but by the world untouched,
Mediate and repeat the name of the Lord Supreme. (Nanak)

9. Sikhism is a modern way of life; it doesn't subject people to rituals or **idol worship**. Sikhism is not about rituals or laws; Sikhism is solely about remembering God.

> **The flowers and leaves that you pluck have life.**
> **But the idol you worship by offering these flowers is lifeless.**
> **Bhagat Kabir-Page 479(SGGS)**

10. Sikhism believes in **Meditation on the True name**. Guru Nanak accepted the path of bhagti, laying emphasis on the worship of the name. To Nanak, *nam* implied not simply the repetition of prayer but prayer with the understanding of words and their translation into action. In Sikh philosophy, the path of *nam* has three ingredients – realization in the heart, its expression in prayer and detachment in all one's actions.

> **"I have no miracles except the name of God," said Nanak**
> **O friends, sing the melodious songs praising the Absolute One God.**
> **O friends by reflecting upon Satguru (God), your desires will be fulfilled.**
> **Guru Arjan Dev Pg. 927 (SGGS)**

11. Sikhism believes in **submitting to the will of God**. When tragedy strikes and there is death and immense sorrow, one must not wail or lament, but sing the praises of the Lord.

12. **Sewa (Service)**. Guru Nanak substituted love in place of all the intricate doctrines of faith. And the practical expression of this love was service. One can see no higher record of service in the annals of mankind than that of the Sikhs, who were taught to

annihilate the thought of self and to utilize all their energies in the service of God and mankind. Discipline of service has played a prominent role in the evolution of the Sikh religion. 'Service' in one form or another is an integral part of a Sikh's duty. Gurudwaras are not only places of worship, but also training centers for service. Such services as sweeping the precincts, serving drinking water to the thirsty, fanning the congregation in hot weather and serving food to the hungry has always formed an integral part of the functions in a Sikh shrine. The Sikh Gurus taught men to earn their future here in this world instead of merely promising unseen bounties in the world to come. Sikhism lays a lot of emphasis on **sewa** (social service). It is the essence of Sikhism. A true Sikh spirit manifests through the Sikh prayers and hymns in the Sikh Sangats (associations), and the serving of food in the Langars to all who sit in the Pangats (rows), which are very essential religio-social services in the Sikh Gurudwaras. "A corporate sense could only arise if certain obligations were made definite and universal, so that the character of a corporate is evolved. It shows why, in spite of the fact that the ideal of service and the inclusion of a spirit of brotherhood were equally significant features of almost all the schools of religious revival in contemporary India, it was in Sikhism alone that a sense of corporate unity gradually evolved. It is important to grasp this because it explains the specialty that arose in Sikhism." (I. B. Bannerji - Evolution of the Khalsa).

13. **The *langar*** (refectory or community kitchen) attached to all Gurudwaras is a fundamental and unique institution of Sikhism. It is a symbol of the Sikh recognition of equality among all people. It fosters among the Sikhs discipline, the spirit of giving and of service. It also instills philanthropy, equality and fraternity. The

Sangat (association) and *pangat* (row or line in which people sit for food in a langar) have a potent influence in the emancipation of the down trodden. These institutions have turned the Sikhs into a classless democratic society. Sikh shrines and other institutions are not only places of worship, but also training centers for service. It is not unusual to see at a langar the landlord or the millionaire seated next to his own servant. Some high-caste may be having his meal along with a Harijan. Cracking jokes and partaking of food at the same place with the local leader may be his chauffeur who drove him there. Attending to the needs of a servant may be his own master.

14. Sikhism **does not believe in conversion**. Forcible conversions or conversions by exploitation are an infringement on human rights.

15. Sikhism strictly **prohibits tobacco**[1] in all its forms (it is absolutely taboo) and it also prohibits wine and other intoxicants.

16. Sikhism **condemns animal sacrifice**, but it does not prohibit the eating of meat. Because of liberal traditions, Sikhs are bound by no strict dogmas or rituals and observe no rigid dos and don'ts in the matter of food. However a devout Sikh refrains from smoking or taking intoxicants and is a strict vegetarian. **By tradition no meat is served in Langars**. Sikhism condemns those as fools who fight over vegetarian and non-vegetarian food, saying that all vegetation has life.

> **Once we say: 'this is pure, this unclean',**
>
> **See that in all things there is life unseen.**
>
> **There are worms in wood and cow dung cakes,**
>
> **There is life in the corn ground into bread,**

There is life in the water which makes it green,

How then be clean when impurity is over the kitchen

spread?

Again

Man is first conceived in flesh, he dewelleth in flesh.

When he quickenth, he obtaineth a mouth of flesh;

his bone, skin, and body are made of flesh.

When he is taken out of the womb, he seizeth teats of flesh.

His mouth is of flesh, his tongue is of flesh, his breath is

in flesh.

When he growth up he marrieth, and bringeth flesh home

with him.

Flesh is produced from flesh; all man's relations are made

from flesh. - NANAK

17. Sikhism believes in **protecting the oppressed and downtrodden**. Sri Guru Gobind was a great revolutionary and humanitarian. He was a social reformer, political rebel and pioneer of nationalism. He motivated people to fight and sacrifice their life and property for the sake of honour, dignity, faith and the motherland. Sikhism believes that the Sikhs should fight for their own rights and also for the rights of others (especially the downtrodden), whenever a wrong, oppression or exploitation takes place.

Recognize him alone as a true and brave warrior,

Who fights for the sake of the poor and oppressed.

And dies, cut piece by piece, but never leaves the field.

- **Bhagat Kabir (Page 1105-SGGS)**

18. Sikhs believe in picking up the sword as a last resort, in order to protect the poor and meek. The Gurus are for a war-free world. But if ever war has to be fought, it is to be fought as a last resort for people's honour. Guru Gobind Singh said, **"All modes of redressing a wrong having failed, raising the sword is just and pious."** If you want peace, you have to be prepared for war.

19. Sikhs believe in **saint-soldiers (sant-sipahi)** and not just mere soldiers. A strict ethical code was laid down when the Sikhs took up arms in 1606. The Geneva Convention (1764) and U. N. O. adopted such codes much later.

20. **Bhai Kanhaiya's**[2] act of serving humanity without any discrimination between friend or foe, even on the battle field, became the precursor of the Geneva Convention of 1764, which granted privileges to the International Red Cross Society for tending to the sick and wounded in war.

21. The Guru Granth Sahib of all the world religious scriptures, alone states that there are **innumerable worlds and universes other than our own.**

> **Numerous worlds there be in the regions beyond the skies and below,**
> **But the search weary scholars say, we do not know.**
> **The Hindu and Muslim books are full of theories;**
> **the answer is but one.**
> **If it be writ , it would have been, but the writer**
> **thereof is none.**
> **O Nanak, say but this, the Lord is great, in His knowledge**
> **He is alone. - Japji (Guru Nanak)**

22. Sikhism might be called the **most materialistic of Indian religions** and history is most important for the Sikhs.

23. Sikhism is perhaps the **most simple, secular, liberal and democratic religion**. All decisions are taken by the will of the majority. There are instances where the Sikhs have ordered the Gurus to obey them. Guru Arjun refused to accept the hand of Chandu Shah's (a Hindu banker) daughter for his son on the decree of the Sikhs. At Chamkaur, when Guru Cobind Singh refused to part from the five remaining Sikhs, he was ordered by the five to make good his escape and a Sikh who resembled the Guru put on his dress and went out to fight. After forming the Khalsa, Guru Gobind Singh asked the panj Pyras (Five beloved ones) to baptize him. After taking amrit, he became a Guru and a disciple (*Ape Gur-chela*).

24. **Neither the ten Gurus were worshipped, nor is the Book (SGGS)**, even though the worshipper will bows or prostrates fully before it. There is sanctity accorded to the Granth and the Sikhs revere it because it contains the writings of their Gurus and other saints they hold in esteem. To them it is more a book of divine wisdom than the word of God. It is the source and not the object of prayer.

> **But whosoever regards me as Lord (god)**
> **Shall be damned and destroyed.**
> **I am – and of this let there be no doubt –**
> **I am but the slave of God, as other men are,**
> **A beholder of the wonders of creation.**
>
> **– Guru Gobind (Bichitra Natak)**

25. Charity and wielding of the sword for a just cause hold a special place in the Sikh Faith. Charity is of all gifts the greatest for it saveth life. The Guru said, "He, who serves the poor and needy, serves me. The mouth of the poor and hungry is the Guru's receptacle of gifts." - (*Graib da Munh Guru Ki Golakh*). The Sword eradicates oppression and tyranny and establishes righteousness. **These two things contributed the most to the popularity and power of the Sikhs and their church.**

26. Simplicity is the hallmark of the Sikh faith, it has simple tenets which disapprove of the caste system and rituals and the only item installed or housed in their gurdwara is the Guru Granth Sahib. The Sikh religion has no priestly order and no sacraments; it is devoid of idols and alters. Any Sikh conversant with the Sikh scriptures can read them. Religion is not the monopoly of any person or class like the priests or pundits.

27. Sikhism is an eco-friendly religion and respects the environment and nature.

   Air is the Guru, Water is the Father, and Earth is the Great Mother of all.

   Day and Night are the two nurses, in whose lap the whole world is at play. - Guru Nanak in Japji Sahib

1. It is known to every Sikh that **tobacco** is forbidden by his religion, but it is not generally known that wine is equally forbidden. After I had quoted the Sikh tenets on this subject in public lectures at Simla, it was taken up by the enlightened Singh Sabha of Patiala; and a resolution in favour of total abstinence was signed by several of the best educated and most influential Sardars of the State.

M.A. Macauliffe in preface to the The Sikh Religion

2. Bhai Kanhaiya (1648-1718*),* founder of **Savapanthi sect** of Sikhs was born in a Dhamman Khatri family of Sodhara near Wazirabad in Sialkot district (now Pakistan). His father was a wealthy trader. Being of a religious bent of mind, he left home at an early age and joined wandering *sadhus* and ascetics in search of spiritual peace. His quest ended when he met Guru Tegh Bahadur and came into the fold of Sikhism. He established a *dharamshala* at Kavha village (Attock district, now in Pakistan), which he turned into a preaching centre. His special mission was selfless service to humanity at large with no discrimination at all. During the Battle of Anandpur (1705), Bhai Kanhaiya happened to be visiting Anandpur. He went around the battle field serving water to the wounded and dying every day without distinction of friend or foe. Some Sikhs complained about him to Guru Gobind Singh. On being questioned, he replied that he saw no Sikhs or Mughals, but the Guru's face in everyone. The Guru was pleased and after blessing him, told him that he had comprehended the teachings of Sikhism profoundly and that he should keep on serving humanity to the best of his ability as long as he could.

After the Battle of Anandpur Bhai Kanhaiya retired to his native place (Sodhara) and passed away in 1718.

The Sewa Panthi tradition flourished in southwest Punjab for nearly 12 generations until 1947. This sect (variously known as Sewa Panthis, Sewa Dassiey, and Addan Shahis), is best symbolized by **Bhai Kanhaiya** who, though himself a Sikh, aided wounded Sikh and Muslim soldiers alike during the Tenth Sikh Guru's wars with the Moghul. Sewa Panthis wore distinctive white robes. This sect thrived in Thal region (Sind Sagar Doab) in what is now Pakistan, near Punjab's boarder with Sind and Baluchistan.

They introduced a new dimension to the sub continental religious philosophies. They believed that sewa (helping the needy) was the highest form of spiritual meditation - higher than singing hymns or reciting holy books. The creation of Pakistan dealt a devastating blow to the Sewa Panthis and they never got truly transplanted in the new "East" Punjab. They are extinct today and it has been an irreparable loss to humanity. An extremely valuable asset was lost for posterity.

Note: A Sikh gurdwara forms the nucleus of the Sikh community life. It performs multifarious functions. It is a school for the student, a spiritual guide for the seekers of the spiritual path, a dispensary for the sick, a grain store and a kitchen for the hungry and a strong fort for the protection of women and additionally an inn and a resting place for the travelers. It is a home away from home.

The doors of Sikh shrines and all other institutions are open to one and all. There is no distinction of religion, caste, creed, colour and sex or rich and poor. The only thing required is to remove shoes, have the head covered and not to carry tobacco and other intoxicants. Those who profess other faiths are as freely allowed to partake of and help in running of langars as the followers of Sikh faith themselves. No distinction is made between man and man, between the Sikhs and non–Sikhs, between high caste and low caste, in seating or serving food in the Guru's kitchen. Men of God, wherever they are, of whatever race or creed, belong to one community, the community of man, free from the chains of birth, creed and race. Sikhism does not believe in the Judgement Day, and respects all faiths. Guru Nanak Devji says,
"There is only one teacher of teachers, who appears in many forms. In whatever house (of faith) the Creator's praises are sung, follow that house, in that house rests true greatness." – SGGS-12.

This great religion of love and peace needs to be explained to the world in the correct perspective because there are a lot of misgivings, wrong conjectures and assumptions about Sikhism. It is regarded as a religion of militancy. Abroad the Sikhs are being mistaken for Muslims and terrorists.

RELATION OF SIKHS WITH MUSLIMS AND HINDUS

Sikhism started as a pacifist, reformist movement. The Sikh faith is by religious origin a purified and protestant development of Hinduism, rejecting idolatry, caste and Brahminical dominance. The essence of Hinduism lies neither in its pantheon of gods nor its social order (caste system), but in its sacred texts – Vedas, Upanishads and Bhagwat Gita. Sikhism was the combination of the teachings of Sufism, which was rooted in Islamic thought and the Bhakti movement, an organic link to Hindu philosophy. The mystical impulse in Sikhism is surely part of what leads some observers to class it with Hinduism, while the explicit monotheism of the tradition resembles that of Islam. Guru Nanak's two permanent life-long companions Bala and Mardana were a Hindu and a Muslim. Nanak emphasized on what was common between the two communities. He proclaimed that the God of the Hindus and Muslims was one and the same God and that all Punjabis were one people because their interests were the same. Sikh hostility to the Muslim was on political basis, while that to the Hindu is on religious basis.

During the first hundred years (1499-1606) approximately i.e. from the time Guru Nanak was ordained in 1499 till the murder of the fifth Guru Arjun Dev by the Mughals in 1606, the first five Gurus preached an egalitarian, monotheistic, non–idolatrous, peaceful order, free of meaningless form or ritual. People flocked to the Sikh fold, because it was simple and practical, it appealed to them, it fired their imagination and the downtrodden came at par with the upper classes.

In the next hundred years (till the formation of the Khalsa in 1699), the Sikhs were forced to become militant in order to fight Mughal tyranny. Guru Tegh Bahadur laid down his life for the protection of the Hindu Dharma and Guru Gobind Singh had to form the Khalsa in order to fight ruthless Mughal oppression. During this period the masses joined the Sikh ranks in order to protect themselves and their families and to evade forcible conversions to Islam.

This period of almost a hundred years from 1606 (the murder of the fifth Guru Arjun Dev) to 1699 (formation of the Khalsa) marked the persecution of the Sikhs. This persecution increased in intensity with the formation of the Khalsa in 1699 and lasted till 1765 (crumbling of the Mughal Empire and ascendancy of the Sikh *Misls*). This duration (1699-1765) is referred to as 'The Period of Repression / Persecution'. Thus the total period of persecution lasted for well over a century and a half. The formation of the Khalsa in fact divided the Sikhs into the Keshdhari/ Amritdhari (ones with unshorn hair who accepted baptism - Khalsa) and the Sehajdhari (those who would take time to adopt the new form) or the Khalsa Sikhs or Singhs and non Khalsa Sikhs. Later the British classified them as Sikhs of Nanak and Sikhs of Gobind. The Keshdhari Sikhs (Khalsa) had to leave there homes and hearths and flee to jungles and deserts in order to save their lives and fight the Mughals and there was a price laid on their heads. The Mughals kept hunting them and the Sikhs kept challenging and defying them. It was at times when the Mughals thought that they had finished the Sikhs, that they rose like the phoenix.

It was during this period that the two *Ghallugharas* (holocausts) took place on 10 March 1746 and 05 February 1762, wherein 7,000 and 25,000 Sikhs (Khalsa) were massacred respectively. The suffering of the Sikhs was tremendous and the mental agony devastating. To live the life of the Khalsa was to be hunted like an animal and was not every one's cup of tea. A vast population of the Hindu faith, during that period, adopted the religion of the Arabian prophet (converted to Islam) as a result of force or with a view to worldly advantage. The majority of Hindus (Sehajdhari Sikhs), who had not joined the Khalsa ranks kept away. However they had a natural affinity for the Khalsa, because in the fate of the Khalsa lay their own interest and survival. They would make one son a Khalsa, help by giving items in cash and kind, and assist in concealing individuals and movements and if they held a high post in the Mughal government; they would extract concessions for the Khalsa through their good offices.

Exactly a hundred years after the formation of the Khalsa in 1699, the Sikhs carved out a Kingdom for themselves in 1799, when Ranjit Singh overpowered and united the *misls* (Sikh confederacies) and was declared the Maharaja of the Punjab and the Khalsa Raj came into existence. During the Khalsa Raj, Maharaja Ranjit Singh ruled with the help of his subjects - Punjabis (Hindus, Muslims and Sikhs alike), irrespective of caste, creed or religion.

With this as the background and for the sake of clarity, it will now be easy to understand the relation of the Sikhs with the Hindus and Muslims.

Sikh – Hindu relations. The religion taught by Nanak was a refined Hinduism purged of its grossness by the more elevated religious precepts of Islam. Sikhism bears to Hinduism much the same relation that Protestantism does to Roman Catholicism, being nothing more than an attempt to free popular Hinduism of its errors and grossness. Hinduism has its huge influence and common concepts with Sikhism and Jainism. The major ones are the Sikh belief in *samsara* (reincarnation) and *karma* (the sum of a person's actions in this and previous lives, seen as affecting their future fate).

The writings of twenty-two Hindus (11 Bhatts and 11 saints - Namdev, Ravidas, Ramanand, Dhanna, Pipa, Jaidev, Trilochan, Beni, Sain, Parmanand and Surdas) are incorporated in the Guru Granth

Sahib. All the Sikh Gurus were Khatri (Hindu sub-caste) Hindus. The vast majority of the followers (Sikhs) of the Gurus also came from the Hindu community. Sikh names, culture, deportment and festivals (Lori, Holi, Basakhi and Deepawali) are similar to the Hindus.

Most Hindu families (especially in N.W. Punjab) brought up one of their sons as a Keshdhari Sikh. They revere the Gurus, read the Guru Granth and intermarried with the Sikhs (more so the Khatri Hindus). Some families of Hindus, even today perform their marriages by Sikh rites. The Hindus of Sind came under the influence of Guru Nanak when he visited Sind and to this day most of them are Sehajdhari Sikhs and have their own Gurdwaras. Majority of Hindus of Punjab and Sind visit both Mandirs and Gurudwaras. These practices continued till recent times and even with the transformation in times, the practices are still common with most families.

During the period of persecution, the Hindus were protected by the Khalsa and in turn they also rendered help by assisting in the war effort in whatever way they could. The majority of Hindus had a soft corner for the Khalsa Sikhs, who were the saviours and defenders of the faith and country. Their own fate, fortunes, safety and religion were intertwined with the Sikhs. And if they held a high post in the Mughal government (like Nand Lal Goya and Kaura Mall), they would extract concessions for the Khalsa through their good offices. On 25 May 1675, a deputation of sixteen Kashmiri Brahmins, headed by Pandit Kirpa Ram[1] came to Guru Teghbahadur with a request to save the Kashmiris from forcible conversion to Islam. The Guru acceded to their request and gave the supreme sacrifice. The services of men like Bhai Nand Lal Goya, Diwan Kaura Mall, Seth Todar Mall[2] and Raja Dina Nath (a Kashmiri pundit, who distinguished himself as one of the ablest and most honest administrators and along with the Fakir Brothers remained loyal to the Lahore Durbar even after the death of Maharaja Ranjit Singh) to the Sikh cause can never be forgotten by the Sikhs. There were also the two Punjabi Hindu generals of Maharaja Ranjit Singh, Mohkam Chand and Misr Dewan Chand who did yeoman service to the Lahore Durbar. The maharaja relied on Diwan Mohkam Chand for advice on military matters and respected him like a father.

The relationship of the Sikhs with the Hindus remained close knit, even when they became a separate community. They really could not free themselves from the shackles of their origins and the dominance of Hindu customs and practices, including those which were in direct contravention to the teachings of their gurus. Though in theory and religion there is no caste system among the Sikhs, but in practice things are quite different. Except for a few stray lines by Guru Gobind Singh there is nothing to substantiate cow-worship in the Sikh scriptures. However the **Sikhs strictly abstain from eating beef and hurting cows** (due to their genesis and intimate links with the religion of their ancestors). During Sikh rule the slaughter of kine was strictly forbidden. The foreigners in the service of Maharaja Ranjit Singh signed contracts not to shave their beards and not to smoke or eat beef. The Namdharis (sub-sect of Sikhs) had forty (40) of their followers blown up by canons (January 1872), during the British Raj, when they murdered some butchers in Malerkotla during their agitation for the protection of cows. Namdharis are ardent protectors of cows and made it the chief point of their agitation against the British. **By tradition no meat is served in Langars**. Although Sikhs are not vegetarians by conviction, the majority eats meat only on rare occasions and a devout Sikh refrains from smoking or taking intoxicants and is a strict vegetarian.

Hinduism is the world's oldest known religion, with its roots going back to 10,000 years and Hindu Literature dating back to 7000 BCE.

Hindu scriptures and knowledge (Yoga, Pranayama, Astrology, Numerology, Palmistry, Vastu, Ayurveda) gained over the ages is praiseworthy. It is very broad and embraces and respects a wide spectrum of beliefs and objects. Parents, Teachers, Environment, Animals, the 9 Planets and the whole Eco-System are quite rightly considered as gods and women are also treated as goddesses. All this makes it an eco-friendly religion with eco-balance profoundly rooted in it. With its origins rooted in antiquity, Hinduism has no known founder, and it is thus a way of life rather than a religion and many things contradict themselves. The sacred texts of Hinduism however remain inviolate.

With the passage of time, some cracks were bound to develop between the two communities that lived in unison and had been bound together by very strong relationships and common interests. The very close affinity of Sikhism with the parent community explains many of the present day contradictions and complexities. The dividing line between the Sikhs and Hindus is very thin.

Differences cropped up when the Arya Samaj established a foothold in Punjab; during the Sikh Gurdwara Movement when the Hindus sided with the Udasi priests; and after partition during the fervent championship of the Punjabi language and agitation for a Sikh state. The happenings of 1984 (the terrible year that changed India forever) added fuel to fire. These include the promoting of Bhindranwale by the Congress in order to oust the Akalis, the demand of a Sikh Homeland, Operation Blue Star and Mrs. Gandhi's assassination. To top it all was the Sikh pogrom of November 1984, followed by ten years of revenge and state oppression in trying to cleanse the Punjab of terrorists. Many innocent lives (mainly Sikh) were lost.

In his book *'The Great Divide'* H. V. Hodson says, "In the light of that history one can imagine Pakistanis thanking heaven that the terms for the transfer of power, by denying Pakistan an undivided Punjab, relieved it of one problem, that of a large, militant, and separatist minority."

Ostensibly the Sikhs feel threatened in a vast ocean of Hinduism. They have the feeling of being discriminated; they fear the disappearance of their separate identity and their absorption in the Hindu fold. They fear religious and economic absorption, in short they fear virtual extinction as a political force; and survival as a rapidly dwindling religious sect of Hinduism. The Sikhs may be doing more harm to themselves than the others are doing to them. They must not forget that times have changed and that they are a minority, their roots lie in Hinduism and their ancestors were all Hindus. The Sikh religion, if not more is at least 50% Hinduism and owes a lot to Hinduism. Even today their customs, practices, culture and life style are deeply embedded in Hinduism, their friends, well-wishers and even relatives are Hindus. Their survival, strength, progress and prosperity lie in education, economic empowerment, tolerance, harmony and peaceful co-existence as taught by their religion. In this respect there is much that they can learn and emulate from the Jews and Parses.

After the Gurdwara Agitation, in which the Hindus supported the Udasi *mahants* (priests), the Sikhs wanted to part ways with the Hindus. The Hindus despite their opposition to the Akalis were magnanimous and continued to protest that the Sikhs were Hindus. They regarded Sikhism as **another branch or a reformed sect of Hinduism** and looked upon it as the **spearhead or militant wing of Hinduism**. Raja Narendra Nath, a leader of the Punjab Hindus while referring to Sikhism as higher Hinduism said: "The Granth Sahib is nothing more or less than the higher teachings of the Vedas and Upanishads in popular language.... I need not dilate upon the close connection between the Hindus and Sikhs; it is well known that of two brothers, one may be a Hindu and another Sikh, and that the Hindus and Sikhs intermarry freely. Khatris and Arora Sikhs living in towns are supposed to follow Hindu law. In this connection it would be interesting to peruse the Privy Council ruling reported as No. 84, P.R., in which the learned judges of the Privy Council held that the Sikhs were Hindus." P.I.C.D., April 5, 1921, p. 539. Another Punjabi Hindu, Sir Gokul Chand Narang, later minister in the Punjab government and author of *Transformation of Sikhism*, who came to the support of the gurdwara legislation, referred to the Sikhs as "flesh of our flesh and the bone of our bone." P.I.C.D., July 6, 1925, p. 539.

Whether the Sikhs were a separate people or a branch of the Hindu social system became a major issue in the years to come. The Punjabi Hindus and Sikhs have very close links; they have a history of co-existence, brotherhood and harmony, emotional connections and enviable cultures and rich traditions and a collective political future and ideological stand points. Despite the ideological divide they have lived together and shared unforgettable memories for decades and centuries. In spite of everything, majority of Punjabi Hindus still consider Sikhs as a sort of Hindu and vice versa. All said and done – **to the majority of Hindus, Sikhs were and are a kind of Hindu, however separate, casteless and dissenting.**

Sikh – Muslim relations. Sikhs believe in one God and in the casteless brotherhood of man. They condemn worship of idols and images. These are only some of the things they have in common with the Muslims. Sikh religion owes much to Sufism and as a system of belief is much closer to Islam than to Hinduism from which it was born. The Sikh and Muslim people are remarkably alike in character and temperament and in the villages of Punjab they lived together in peaceful co-existence; had similar ways of life and a common cultural heritage to share.

As believers in a revealed religion of one God, as foes of caste and the worship of idols, who had to fight for their religious creed against the pervading pantheism of Hindu India, it might be thought that they had much in common with the followers of Mohamed. However as with the Muslims themselves in their reaction to the Hindu Raj, it was not the niceties of religious dogma but the call of historical memories that stirred the Sikhs as the prospect of democratic rule and division of India drew near.

Three centuries of persecution and fighting have made the two communities hostile to each other. The Sikhs were hunted, butchered and all kinds of horrible and unimaginable atrocities were committed on them. There were genocides, holocausts and ethnic cleansing. Thus the Muslim became the traditional enemy of the Sikh and at the time of partition he was the actual enemy. Nevertheless if there were tyrants and a large number of Muslims with animosity towards the Sikhs, there were a few Muslims with good will too, who had a close association with Sikhs. Some of them were Mardana (a Mirasi i.e. a caste of minstrels and genealogists, who was a life-time companion of Guru Nanak), Hazrat Mian Mir (a Sufi saint of the Qadiriyah order, who is said to have laid the foundation stone of Harimandar Sahib and was also instrumental in securing the release of Guru Hargobind from Gwalior Fort, where he was detained under Jahangir's orders), Nabi Khan and Ghani Khan (the two Muslims who carried Guru Gobind in a curtained palanquin in the guise of Uch da Pir and helped him get past the Mughal sentries at Machiwara, after the battle of Chamkaur and make good his escape) and Pir Buddhu Shah[3]. There are writings of seven (07) Muslim saints (Farid, Kabir, Sadhna, Bikhan, Mardana, Satta and Balwand) in the Guru Granth Sahib.

During Maharaja Ranjit Singh's time his closest confidant was his foreign minister, a Muslim by the name of Faqir Azizuddin (he was of Sufi persuasion and thus had no prejudice against other religions). The Maharaja consulted him in all matters concerning the state and rarely undertook any decision without his consent. His younger brother Fakir Nuruddin was the Maharaja's home minister as well as the royal physician and custodian of the key to the royal treasury. He commanded Ranjit Singh's arsenal at the Lahore Fort. Apart from this, he was also responsible for commissioning arts all over India. As a result, the period of Sikh rule witnessed a flourishing of art. A third brother Fakir Imamuddin, on the other hand, was the custodian of the Gobindgarh fort in Amritsar, where Ranjit Singh kept most of the munitions of war. The three Fakirs were, without doubt, the Maharaja's most loyal men. They remained loyal to Ranjit Singh to the very end of his life and even after that, they severed the Lahore Durbar right till the time, the English took over the kingdom of the Sikhs. Another Muslim officer, Mian Ghausa and after him General Ilahi Bakhsh was in charge of the Artillery and the police administration of the capital Lahore was in the hands of a Muslim officer, Imam Baksh. It was the Muslim troops of Maharaja Ranjit Singh, led by Colonel Sheikh Baswan (a Muslim officer) that forced the Khyber Pass and carried the Maharaja's colours through the streets of Kabul in the victory parade in 1839 (the year Ranjit Singh died).

Faqir Azizuddin, who led a Punjabi delegation to Lord William Bentinck at Simla in 1831, was asked by an officer of the governor general in which eye Ranjit Singh was blind. "The splendour of his face is such," replied the Fakir, "that I have never been able to look close enough to discover." Today a large part of the collection in the private Museum of the descendants of the Fakir Brothers named *The Fakir Khana Museum* at Lahore consists of gifts given to the Fakirs by Ranjit Singh. Fakir Syed Waheeduddin a descendant of Faqir Azizuddin wrote a wonderful 280 page book 'The Real Ranjit Singh' in 1981. The book became very popular and was republished in January 2001 by Punjabi University Patiala. The descendants of the Fakir Brothers eulogize the great Maharaja to this day.

A Muslim, **Tarek Fatah** from Pakistan has this to say about Sikhism and its association with Islam, "It (Partition) is sad because Sikhism and Guru Nanak were intertwined with Islam and Muslims. The Guru's closest companion was a Muslim by the name of Bhai Mardana. It is said when Mardana was dying, the Guru asked him, how would you like to die? Would it be as a Muslim? To which the ailing companion replied, "As a human being." Before 1947, Punjabi Muslims did not consider Sikhism as an adversarial faith. After all, from the Muslim perspective, Sikhism was the combination of the teachings of Sufism, which was rooted in Islamic thought and the Bhakti movement, an organic link to Hindu philosophy. It is true that Moghul emperors had been particularly vicious and cruel to the leaders of the Sikh faith, but these Moghuls were not acting as representatives of Islam. Not only that, the Moghuls inflicted even harsher punishments on their fellow Muslims."

It was indeed as recognition of the common cultural heritage of its people irrespective of religious community that a Pakistan Embassy official once remarked to a Sikh political leader during negotiations to allow more Sikhs to visit Nankana Sahib (the birth place of Nanak): **'He was born with us. Only you have taken him over.'** – Page 235 Robber Noblemen by Joyce Pettigrew.

Every year on Guru Nanak's birthday, the descendents of Bhai Mardana come from Pakistan to the Golden Temple to sing the hymns of Guru Nanak. Before partition i.e. August 1947, in any gathering in a Gurudwara the inmates comprised of 75-80% Sikhs and Hindus and about 20-25% Punjabi Muslims. After the proceedings were over the Muslims would request for the shloks (hymns or verses) of Baba Farid to be sung. The partition alienated them and they broke away from the Sikhs. It was a sad ending indeed.

When human beings live together, conflict is inevitable. War is not. - Daisaku Ikeda

1. Pandit Kirpa Ram, (d. 1705) was a Kashmiri pundit who had met and sought the blessings of Guru Har Rai, at the time of the latter's visit to Kashmir. In May 1675, Kirpa Ram led a delegation of Kashmiri pundits to Guru Tegh Bahadur in order to request him to save the Kashmiri Hindus from forcible conversion to Islam. Later after the martyrdom of Guru Tegh Bahadur, he became a Sikh under the influence of Guru Gobind Singh and fell a martyr in the battle of Chamkaur. To this day his descendants are turbaned Sikhs. According to some chronicles, Pandit Kirpa Ram helped Guru Gobind Singh in his Sanskrit education.

2. Seth Todar Mall, a wealthy merchant of Sirhind, who performed the last rites of the two younger sons of Guru Gobind Singh martyred, on 12 December 1706, under the orders of Wazir Khan, faujdar of Sirhind, and of Mata Gujari, the Guru's mother who died of shock on the same day. It is said that landowners around the Sirhind Fort would not permit him (Seth Todar Mall) to cremate the bodies in their fields, until one Chaudhari Atta agreed to sell him a plot. The condition laid by the Choudhari was that Seth Todar Mall could take only that much land which he could cover with gold coins (*mohars*). The Seth covered the ground that he needed with gold coins and cremated the three dead bodies. The ashes of the bodies was put in an urn and buried at the site of cremation. Gurdwara Joti Sarup stands at this location today. Modern historians trying to trace the antecedents of Seth Todar Mall say that he was the son or later descendant of Raja Todar Mall, of Sirhind, who won renown as an administrator under the Mughal emperors, Shah Jahan and Aurangzeb, and who, according to Shah Nawaz Khan, *Maasir ul-Umara*, lived up to 1076 AH/AD 1666. In order to commemorate the noble deed of this august gentleman, Seth Todar Mall, a road in Sirhind town and a hall in Gurdwara Fatehgarh Sahib have been named after him.

3. Pir Buddhu Shah (1647 – 1704), a Muslim divine whose real name was Badr ud-Din. He was an admirer of Guru Gobind Singh. Because of his simplicity and silent nature during childhood, he was given the nickname Buddhu (literally simpleton). In 1685, at Paonta, on his recommendation the Guru engaged 500 Pathan soldiers under the command of four leaders, Kale Khan, Bhikhan Khan, Nijabat Khan and Hayat Khan. In 1688, when Guru Gobind Singh was attacked by a combined force of the hill chiefs led by Raja Fateh Shah of Srinagar (Garhwal), all the Pathans with the exception of Kale Khan deserted him and joined hands with the hill monarch. The news of the treachery was sent to the Pir. He immediately rushed to the battlefield of Bhangani, with his brother, four sons and 700 of his followers. The battle was won, but at a very heavy cost. Pir Buddhu Shah lost his brother Bhure Shah, two sons Ashraf and Muhammad Shah and many of his disciples.

The rich presents offered to the Pir after the battle by Guru Gobind Singh were politely declined by him. He however requested the Guru for the kangha (comb) stuck in his hair and the turban that he was about to tie. Guru Gobind Singh granted his wish and gave him the two articles along with a small *kirpan*. The Pir and his descendants kept these items in their family as sacred heirlooms until Maharaja Bharpur Singh of Nabha (1840 - 63) acquired them in exchange for a *jagir* (land grant).

Complaints about the Pir regarding the assistance that he had rendered to Guru Gobind Singh reached the imperial government at Delhi. The *faujdar* of Sirhind ordered Usman Khan to deal with Pir Buddhu Shah. The Pir was arrested at Sadhaura (Ambala district), his home town and executed on 21 March 1704. The great Sikh General Banda Singh Bahadur avenged the Pir's execution in 1709 by storming Sadhaura and killing Usman Khan. Pir Buddhu Shah's descendants migrated to Pakistan in 1947. Their ancestral house in Sadhaura has been converted into a Gurdwara named after Pir Buddhu Shah. It will also be worth mentioning here that a *palang* (bed) gifted to Guru Gobind Singh by Pir Buddhu Shah is placed in the Singh Sabha Gurdwara at Jodhpur.

Note 1 - Most Hindu **Sindhis** and **Punjabis** and certain sects, whether you call them **Sahijdharis**, half Hindu half Sikh or by some other name, believe in the Gurus and Guru Granth Sahib, but the majority **do not** take the Khalsa baptism, keep unshorn hair and tie turbans or add Singh/Kaur to their name. Many believe in a living guru. These sects include the **Nirankari** and **Radha Soamis**; **Udasis** founded by Sri Chand (1494-1629), son of Guru Nanak; **Sewapanthis** founded by Bhai Kahnaiya or perhaps Bhai Sewa Ram; the **Ramraiyas**, followers of Ram Rai (1646-1687), the eldest son of Guru Har Rai; the **Minas**, followers of Prithi Chand (1558-1618), the eldest son of Guru Ram Rai; the **Handalis** or **Niranjanis** founded by Handal (1573-1646); the **Gulabdasias** (an epicurean sect) founded by one Pritam Das; the **Nanakpanthis**, **Kabirpanthis**, **Satnamis** (three religious bodies had this name),

Raidasis/Ravdasis and other sects of minor importance. The majority of them goes to both mandir and gurdwara and worship Hindu gods alongside the *Granth* and follow other Hindu practices and the majority of them write their religion as Hindu. **Dera Sacha Sauda** is another sect of comparatively recent origin (founded in April 1948) by a Sikh Baba, Beparvah Mastana. The Dera claims to believe in humanity as the greatest religion and accordingly professes to be involved in the service of humanity. Dera Sacha Sauda, the Nirankaris and Radha Soamis have a vast followings in India and abroad.

Then there are the Namdharis and Nirmalas; they generally keep unshorn hair and tie turbans and are more Sikh than Hindu, but they observe some Hindu beliefs, rituals and customs too. The **Namdharis** believe in the motto 'back to the simplicity and pristine glory of Sikhism.' They have a living guru, revere the cow and have mass marriages with no expenditure or dowry. The **Nirmalas** generally do not take the Khalsa baptism, don ochre or saffron coloured garments, mostly practice celibacy and are devoted to scriptural and philosophical studies. By tradition they are inclined towards classical Hindu philosophy especially Vedanta. They have mastery over the Sanskrit language and the Vedas. Their contribution towards the preaching of Sikh doctrine and production of philosophical literature in Sanskrit, Braj, Hindi and Punjabi is considerable. They have *Akharas* (monastery/seminary) in all major Hindu centers – Kankhal, Haridwar, Varanasi (Kashi), Allahabad (Prayag) and also in Punjab. They also take out their own *raths* (carriage pulled by horses) during the *kumbh Melas*.

Note 2 During the rise of *misls* and when the Sikhs attained power, a large number of Hindus accepted conversion to Sikhism (Khalsa), which they regarded as **another branch or reformed sect of Hinduism** and looked upon it as the **spearhead or militant wing of Hinduism**. Large number of Hindu Jats (peasants) also joined the militant Khalsa and so drew the Sikhs closer to the Hindus. These people brought customs and prejudices with them and considerably altered the faith of Nanak and the gurus. Ceremonies and rituals, which already existed due to the Udasis gained strength in the Sikh Gurdwaras and the Brahmins again, gained influence and re-introduced caste prejudices and cow-worship. There was a serious decline in moral standards especially among the Sikh aristocracy, which was largely Jat and began to look upon itself as the Kshatriya and aped the practices of Hindu Rajput princes. During Sikh rule the distinction between Sikh and Hindu became one of mere form; the Khalsa wore their hair and beards unshorn, the Hindus did not.

When the British conquered Punjab John Lawrence, who was a member of the Board of Control made the Sikhs repeat loudly: "*Bevi mat jalao*"- Do not burn widows. "*Beti mat maro*" – Do not kill daughters. "*Korhi mat dabao*" – Do not bury lepers. (Bosworth Smith, *Life of Lord Lawrence*, I, 206). Little did the English know that all this and much more was given in the Sikh Religion and also little did they know that the illiterate Sikhs (for them warfare and not religion entailed employment and survival) did not know their own religion. Later the British became more aware of the Sikh Religion and it was left to the Singh Sabha to educate and teach the Sikhs their own religion. It must also be noted that today the Jat Sikhs are the longest adherents to the Sikh faith.

Note 3 – True, there was indeed a time in the *Sanatan*, Sikh world when Udasi, Seva Panthi and Nirmala Gurdwaras, Deras, Ashrams, Dhramsalas etc. (places of worship) kept Sikh scriptures, along with Muslim and Hindu scriptures. Within the spiritual halls sermons of common humanity, spirituality and love of the all mighty were given from all these sacred texts to the Sikh, Hindu and Muslim, congregation. Right into the 50s and early 60s of the last century, the Sikhs wrote their religion as Sikh with Hindu in parentheses -- Sikh (Hindu); a very small minority still follows this practice today. These are perhaps some of the things which certain above mentioned sects are trying to emulate and exploit today.

APPENDICES

SIKH POPULATION ABROAD

TOP TEN CITIES IN US, CANADA AND ENGLAND WITH A LARGE SIKH POPULATION

OCTOBER, 2014 AT 19:49

1) City: Surrey, Canada (Largest Sikh Settlement Outside of Punjab) (120,000 Sikhs)
   Sikhs as a Percentage of total Population: 42%

2) City: Richmond Hill, NY
   Sikhs as Percentage of Total Population: 38%

3) City: Millbourne, PA USA
   Sikhs as a Percentage of Total Population: 36%

4) City: Brampton, Canada
   Sikhs as a Percentage of Total Population: 24%

5) City: Abbotsford, Canada
   Sikhs as a Percentage of Total Population: 19%

6) City: Slough, UK
   Sikhs as a Percentage of Total Population: 12%

7) City: Yuba City California, USA   Sikhs as a Percentage of Total Population: 11%

8) City Wolverhampton, UK
   Sikhs as a Percentage of Total Population: 10.2%

9) City: Hounslow, UK
   Sikhs as a Percentage of Total Population: 10%

10) City: Ealing, UK

    Sikhs as a Percentage of Total Population: 8.5%

Notables:

City: Glasgow, Scotland, UK
Sikhs as a Percentage of Total Population: 4%

City: Ieicester, UK
Sikhs as a Percentage of Total Population: 4%

As for total Population in Canada of Sikhs: Surrey (120,000 Sikhs), Brampton, Ontario (98,000) and Calgary, Alta (29,000) has a higher population than Abbotsford. Abbotsford has 26,000 Sikhs while Vancouver has 17,000 and Toronto has 20,000.

Other Notes

To put things in perspective, Sikhs - now numbering well over half a million in Canada - are by far the biggest group among those hailing, or descending from immigrants, from the subcontinent. Since they were the first group from the area to land in Canada's British Columbia province in the last decade of the 19th century, it is not surprising that Sikhs made history in Canada when Ujjal Singh Dosanjh was elected as the premier of British Columbia in Feb. 2000. Today there are 17 Sikh MPs and four Sikh Canadian ministers in Mr Trudeau's Cabinet including two ladies – Joginder 'Jinny' Kaur Sims and Neena Kaur Grewal. In contrast, there are three Sikh Cabinet ministers in the Modi government - Maneka Gandhi, who is a Sikh by birth, Harsimrat Kaur Badal who is the Food Processing Minister and the recently inducted minister of state Mr Ahluwalia. Of late another Sikh gentleman – Mr Hardeep Puri has been included as the Urban Development Minister. There are 13 Sikh MPs in the Indian parliament.

TOP TWENTY COUNTRIES WITH A LARGE SIKH POPULATION

OCTOBER, 2014 AT 19:49

1. INDIA 215,00,000 2%

2. CANADA 4, 68,673 1.4%

3. UK 4,32,000 .8%

4. USA 2,50,000 .08%

5. MALAYSIA 1,00,000 .37%

6. AUSTRALIA 72,296 .12%

7. ITALY 70,000 .11%

8. THAILAND 70,000 .1%

9. KENYA,UGANDA 50,000-1,00,000 .64% And TANZANIA

10. MAURITIUS 37,700 .3%

11. GREECE 20,000 .11%

12. KUWAIT 20,000 .64%

13. PAKISTAN 20,000 .01%

14. NEW ZEALAND 19,191 .43%

15. INDONESIA 15,000 .1%

16. GERMANY 12 - 40,000 .01%

17. NETHERLANDS 12,000 .07%

18. FRANCE 10,000 .02%

19. BELGIUM 10,000 .09%

20. MEXICO 8,000 .3%

THE WHITE SIKHS

The **'White/Gora Sikhs'** in America, Canada and Europe follow Sikhism in toto. They first started following the Sikh religion after becoming the followers of Yogi Harbhajan. Their number, today, is estimated to be approximately fifty thousand.

This is a **list of some prominent white converts to Sikhism**.

Sikhism does not favour proselytizing or vigorous conversion campaigns, but allows people to follow the religion according to their own will. Anyone interested in adopting Sikhism is free to do so irrespective of gender, race or ethnicity.

- Alexandra Aitken - actress and daughter of former British cabinet minister Jonathan Aitken

- Vic Briggs - former blues musician who converted and took the name Vikram Singh Khalsa; became the first non-sub-continental to perform kirtan at Harimandir Sahib.

- Peggy Ferrar DiCaprio - actress; wife of writer George DiCaprio; stepmother of actor Leonardo DiCaprio.

- Vikram Kaur Khalsa - former model and actress, who starred in several horror movies.

- Max Arthur Macauliffe (1841–1913) - senior British administrator who was posted in the Punjab; prolific scholar and author; converted to Sikhism in the 1860s.

- Babaji Singh - credited with translating Guru Granth Sahib, the holy text of the Sikhs, into Spanish.

- Martin Singh - Nova Scotia pharmacist and businessman and candidate for the leadership of the New Democratic Party of Canada in 2012.

- Ocean Singh - _MTV Roadies_; born a Hindu and embraced Sikhism after learning the basic concepts of the faith; stated in his audition that Sikhism appealed to him due to the importance of being a soldier and saint.

- Dharma Singh Khalsa - medical researcher in the field of Alzheimer's disease.

- Mahan Atma Singh Khalsa - formerly Andy Strachan; guitarist and member of the band DYS; co-founded the band Slaughter Shack; after leaving music, converted to Sikhism.

2

SIKH POPULATION IN INDIA

A number of Sikhs and others associated with or concerned about Sikhs in various ways have shown concern over the numbers of Sikhs being projected in the Indian demographic census. They say that the number of Sikhs is much higher than being shown in the census of the country. And some even go to the extent of putting the Sikh population at around 13 crore instead of 2 crore. The population of Sikh tribes includes Sikligars, Vanjaras, Assamese, Tharu and a large number of Nanak Panthis. Some of these may be a floating population and others may not like to identify with the Sikhs because of the fear of being isolated or segregated in a vast ocean of people, among whom they live and are a minuscule minority. These Sikhs have remained neglected over the ages, which have separated them from the main stream. Their condition is miserable and they are living in abject poverty and because of their condition, other religious agencies are exploiting them by either converting them or making them count among their numbers. It is high time the Sikhs woke up to the situation and did something to improve their condition and bring them back to main stream Sikhism.

Guru Amar Das, the third Guru established 22 *Manjis* (parishs or dioceses) all over the country and appointed some leading Sikhs to cater to the needs of Sikh sangats (gathering of Sikh fraternity) in the districts or areas, where people had become the followers of Sikhism after the visit of Guru Nanak and other Gurus. The dharamsalas/deras/gurdwaras in these *Manjis* were manned by *Udasi* or *Nirmala* saints along with *masands* (agents) who collected offerings of *dasvandh* (tithe) and carried it to the Gurus. When the *masands* became corrupt Guru Gobind Singh abolished the institution of *masands* and asked the Sikhs to communicate directly with him without intermediaries.

Sikhs in Other States. In Bihar and Jharkhand there are old historic gurdwaras and pockets of very old Sikh concentrations in Patna, Gaya and Sasaram; similarly such concentrations exist in Rajasthan, Maharashtra, Andhra Pradesh, Assam and many other parts of the country. It is these Sikhs, all over the country, that have been following Sikhism for centuries, who are suffering the most because with the passage of time they have been completely cut off, from main stream Sikhism. During the anti-Sikh riots of 1984, they suffered the maximum. The Sikh concentration of farmers in Terai (U.P.), Ganganagar (Rajasthan), Kutch (Gujrat) and some other places are of recent origin.

The Partial Sikhs. There is also a substantial population that is half Hindu-half Sikh; some of them may address themselves as Hindus and the others Sikhs; they are mostly Sahajdhari Sikhs from among the Khatri, Arora and Sindhi urban community who for ages have been intermarrying among their own community of Hindus and Sikhs; today they are turning away because of the rigid stance being adopted by the S.G.P.C. The majority of them are Nanak Panthis and once they did follow all Sikh practices (except the 5 Ks of the *Khalsa*) and even made the eldest son of the family a *keshdhari/Khalsa* Sikh. In present times they are shying away and barring a few, the majority is more Hindu than Sikh and profess their religion to be Hindu. A few of these people of this Sahajdhari Sikh community write Sikh as their religion and in brackets (parenthesis) Hindu. The Nanak Panthis, Kabir Panthis, Ravdasias, Nirankaris, Radha Soamis and various *Dera* followers like Dera Sacha Sauda also read and preach from the Guru Granth Sahib in a big way, but the majority of them write their religion as Hindu.

Sikhs who forgot their roots. In the belt between Delhi and Moradabad, there lie about 100 odd villages, established by Sikhs during the *Misl* Period. These Sikhs were sent by various *misls*, to protect the people in this area, when they pleaded for help and protection against the atrocities of the Mughals. But sadly with the passage of time these Sikhs have become more Jat than Sikh, they have even forgotten their mother tongue. What remains of them are old nostalgic memories; you can often hear some of them say, "My grandfather or great grandfather was a Sikh."

Kuchesar It may also be worth mentioning (for information/ knowledge) that two hours away from Delhi, at a distance of 80 kms, in Bulandshahr district (Uttar Pradesh), lies a small princely state or a seat of Jagirdari (Zamidari), called **Kuchesar**. Kuchesar is a Jat state, famous for the mud fort at Kuchesar and the rulers belong to the **Dalal** clan of Jats. The Kuchesar Fort was brought into the ruling family's possession in the eighteenth century when the Mughal emperor Najib ud-Dawlah bestowed the Jat family with the title of Rao Bahadur and the Jagir of Kuchesar comprised 365 villages. Rao Chhatar Singh was the first Rao of Kuchesar.

The tenth (10th) and last ruler, **Rao Bahadur Giriraj Singh** (20 September 1877–1943), succeeded to the *gadi* or throne on 03 June 1898 and was granted the title of Rao Bahadur on 3rd June 1918. He became a devoted Sikh under the influence of his wife **Rani Rajbans Kaur** who belonged to the house of **Bhadaur** (a Phulkian princely estate 25 km northwest of Barnala in Sangrur district of Punjab). The descendants of Rao Bahadur Giriraj Singh follow Sikhism to this day. **Rao Bahadur Indarjit singh** (b. 15 October 1894) became the 11th Rao of Kuchesar in 1943 and his son **Ajit Singh** is the present head of the family. Part of the Kuchesar Fort is now two heritage hotels; one is **Mud Fort Kuchesar** and the other **Rao Raj Vilas**. Kuchesar is counted among the Jat Kingdoms and only the ruling family is Sikh. This fact is perhaps unknown to the majority of Sikhs.

Similarly the ruling family of the erstwhile **Purnia state** in Bihar has also been Nanakpanthi and still has a gurdwara in their palace. Another interesting fact is that a village **Ghail** (Ambala District) is a village of banayas who, are keshdhari Sikhs.

 Lastly the most important factor that will accrue profit out of proportion to all efforts put in is that non-Punjabi Sikhs and the so-called Sikh tribes are in greater numbers than Sikhs in the Punjab. This large number shall ultimately enrich and strengthen the Sikh community. Such an effort would also add to the Sikh demographic figures - always needed in a democratic set-up of governance. The population of the Sikhs will increase substantially. The Sikhs will have more representation in parliament and make their voice heard. These people will act as ambassadors of the faith in far flung areas where Sikhs are unseen and unheard of. The Sikhs just cannot afford to lose these people. It will be an irreparable loss that the community cannot afford. By helping these people (the Sikh people and not outsiders), the Sikhs tend to benefit a lot. If help does not come forth from the Sikh community, these people will seek assistance elsewhere and there are communities more than willing to exploit the situation and take advantage of their condition. So it would be a gross mistake to ignore the writing on the wall and the lessons of history. What the Sikhs forget is that it the voice of the people, the majority and the numbers that count in a democratic country.

3

BOOKS AND WRITINGS ON SIKHISM BY BENGALI AUTHORS

There was an influx of Bengali intellectuals in Punjab during the latter half of the nineteenth century. The Bengalis preached liberal Hinduism of **Raja Ram Mohan Roy** (1771-1833) and the **Brahmo Samaj** (founded by Raja Ram Mohan Roy in 1828). There were a lot of similarities between the teachings of Sikhism and Brahmo Samaj. Many *Brahmo Mandirs* and Shantiniketan recite from the Sikh scriptures and Brahmo Samaj Sangeet i.e. their hymns include many *shabads* of Guru Nanak. Guru Nanak Dev *ji's* birthday is celebrated even now in Shantiniketan with *Deepmala* and *Aarti* in Bengali.

There is a lot of Sikh literature written by Bengali authors in Bengali and English. Many works including the Guru Granth have been translated into Bengali. The father and son duo of Maharishi Debendranath and Rabindranath Tagore (Nobel Laureate) who were followers of Brahmo Samaj were greatly influenced by Sikhism. They visited Amritsar and the Golden Temple a number of times. Rabindranath Tagore had a life long association with Sikhism and its history as depicted in his writings and poems on Sikh themes. Here are some names of the works produced by Bengali authors:

1. **Bandi Bir** (Warrior Bound) is a poem in Bengali by Rabindranath Tagore, based primarily on McGregor's *History of the Sikhs* and Cunningham's *A History of the Sikhs*. It was composed by him in October-November 1899. The poem celebrates the heroism of the Sikh warrior Banda Singh Bahadur (1670-1716). The opening stanzas tell how Guru Gobind Singh's message had turned the Sikhs into a self-respecting and fearless people.

152

2. **Bir Guru** by Rabindranath Tagore (1861-1941), is a life sketch in Bengali of Guru Gobind Singh (1666-1708), emphasizing especially how he had prepared the Sikhs to stand up to oppression and injustice. This is Tagore's first writing on Guru Gobind Singh published in 1885. The poet was then in his early twenties and seems to be well conversant with Sikh history.

3. **Guru Gobinda** is one of Rabindranath Tagore's three poems in Bengali on Guru Gobind Singh. The poem depicts Guru Gobind Singh as a selfless national leader. The other two poems are "Nishfal Uphar" (A Selfless Gift) and "Shesh Shiksha" (The Last Lesson). The three poems were composed by Tagore sometime between June 1888 and October 1899.

4. **Prarthanatita Dan**, poem in Bengali by Rabindranath Tagore on the Sikh martyr Bhai Taru Singh. Written on 18-19 November 1899; it was included in *Katha*, a collection of Tagore's poems published in October-November 1899.

5. **Guru Gobinda**, by Harnath Bose, first published in 1908, is a play written in colloquial Bengali literary tradition, with Guru Gobind Singh as the hero.

6. **Guru Gobind Singha**, by Basanta Kumar Banerjee, is a biography in Bengali of Guru Gobind Singh. The book was first published in 1909 and later translated into Hindi and English.

7. **Guru Gobind Singha**, by Jogendranath Gupta, is a brief life-sketch in Bengali, of Guru Gobind Singh. This booklet of 53 pages was published in 1923 and is meant for school children.

8. **Guru Gobind Singh**, by Tinkari Banerjee, is a biography in Bengali of Guru Gobind Singh. The book was first published in 1896, then in

1918 (this edition contains more information on the Guru) and the last edition was further improved with portraits and maps. In the book, the author depicts wholehearted admiration and reverence for the Guru.

9. **Maharajaraja Ranjit Singh Jiban Vrittani** is a monogram written by Brahmamohan Mallick in Bengali and published in 1862.

10. **Nanak**, by Ksitish Chakravarty, is a versified biography of Guru Nanak (1469-1539) in Bengali. The book was published in 1916. The poet refers solely to Annie Basant's *Children of the Motherland* as his sources of reference, but it seems that he was not wholly unaware of some of the writings on Sikhs published in the *Bharati* and other contemporary Bengali journals.

11. **Nanak Prakash**, by Bhai Mahendranath Bose, is a biography of Guru Nanak in the Bengali language. The author was a follower of Keshabchandra Sen, and the followers of Sen used the word *Bhai* or Rev. *Bhai* for one another to convey a sense of close kinship and brotherhood. The first part of the book was published in 1885 and the second in 1893.

12. **Sikh**, a play by Bipinbihari Nandi published in Bengali in 1909, traces the consolidation of the Sikhs as Khalsa under Guru Gobind Singh.

13. **Sikh**, by Rajnikanta Gupta, is a brief monograph in Bengali on the history of the Sikhs from Guru Nanak (1469-1539) to the conquest of the Punjab by the British in 1849.

14. **Sikher Balida**, by Kumudin Mitra, first published in 1904, is a small tract, in Bengali language, of forty-one pages, dealing with the heroic sacrifices of seven Sikh martyrs. Perhaps inspired by Rabindranath Tagore's poems on Banda Singh Bahadur and Bhai Taru Singh, she introduced five more martyrs to the Bengali readership.

15. **Sikher Katha** (*katha*, i.e. story, of the Sikhs), by Jatinderanath Samaddar, published in 1912, is a five-act drama, in Bengali language, dealing primarily with the life and work of Guru Gobind Singh.

16. **Sikh Guru o Sikh Jati**, by Sarat Kumar Roy, is a brief history in Bengali of the Sikhs from the birth of Guru Nanak (1469-1539), founder of the faith, to the fall of the Sikh kingdom in 1849. The book was first published in 1909, and reprinted in 1921.

17. **Evolution of the Khalsa** (two volumes), by Indubhusan Banerjee, in English. Vol. 1 was published in 1935 and Vol. 2 in 1947. Both the volumes cover the Guru period from 1469-1708. This was the first work on Sikh history, written, by a Bengali intellectual, purely in a historical discipline. His Evolution of the Khalsa can be regarded as one of the most influential scholarly work of the first half of twentieth century and up to the end of twentieth century it dominated the curriculum of history in the universities of the Punjab.

18. **Military System of the Sikhs** is an English book written by Lt. Col. B. N. Majumdar B.A., LLB. PSC. The book was first published in 1965.

Jaidev was a Bengali Brahmin and the author of the famous **Gita Govinda**. Two of his poems are contained in the Guru Granth.

Sat Sabha, a religious and social reform society founded at Lahore by a group of two Bengalis, Babu Novin Chandra Rai and S.P. Bhattacharjee and two Punjabi Hindus, Pandit Bhanu Datta Basant Ram and Lala Behari Lal Puri. In the sphere of religion, the Sat Sabha preached an eclectic theism, very similar in content to that professed by the Lahore Brahmo Samaj and also worked in the social field like the Brahmo Samaj. The major difference between the Sat Sabha and the Brahmo Samaj lay in the area of language. The Brahmo Samaj published its literature in either English or Hindi. The Sat Sabha, by contrast made the encouragement of Punjabi in the Gurmukhi script one of its major goals. The Sat Sabha's advocacy of Punjabi made it one of the few groups outside the Sikh community to espouse this language in the debates of the late nineteenth century.

Led by Behari Lal, the secretary of the Sabha, they debated and argued in favour of Punjabi. Behari Lal's reputation as a poet and composer of popular *bhajans* strengthened his advocacy of the Punjabi language. The second major leader of the Sat sabha was Pandit Bhanu Datta Basant Ram, the Acharya of the society. He played a prominent role in the religious debates among Punjabi Hindus and even opposed the Arya Samaj when Swami Dayanand came to Lahore in 1877. Throughout its history, the Sabha continued to be seen as a "Brahmic institution, whose object is to inculcate pure Theistic worship." Even though the Sabha did not become a mass movement like the Arya Samaj and remained confined to Lahore, it proved a centre for discussion and debate during the latter years of the nineteenth century. The Sat Sabha remains in Punjab history as an early example of social and religious reform stemming directly from the cultural influence of the Brahmo Samaj, but in a particularly Punjabi form tied to the advancement of the Punjabi language.

4

ARTI BY GURU NANAK

Once actor Balraj Sahni asked the Nobel Laureate Rabindra Nath Tagore, "You have written the National Anthem for India, can you write an International anthem for the whole world?"

"It has already been written not only internationally, but for the entire universe, in the 16th century by Nanak," replied Tagore. He referred To the Sikh *Arti* (adoration of God by a ceremony of lights). Gurudev Tagore was so enamoured of this *arti* that he personally translated it into Bengali.

As legend has it, in 1508 CE Guru Nanak Dev visited the famous temple of Jagannath at Puri in Orissa, which was very well known for its *arti* for Lord Krishna. In the evening, priests brought a platter full of many lighted lamps, flowers, incense and pearls and began the *arti*…

Guru Nanak Sahib meanwhile spontaneously gave words to the wonderful *arti* which was being hummed by Nature before the invisible altar of God, the creator of this universe.

Raag Dhanaasree, First Mehl:

*(Upon that cosmic
plate of the sky,
the sun and the moon
are the lamps. The stars
and their orbs are the
studded pearls)*

फूलंत *joti* ॥१॥

*(The fragrance of sandalwood
in the air is the temple incense,
and the wind is the fan. All the
plants of the world are the altar
flowers in offering to You,
O Luminous Lord)*

*(What a beautiful Aartee,
lamp-lit worship service this is!)*

*(O Destroyer of Fear, this is
Your Ceremony of Light)*

*(The Unstruck Sound-current
of the Shabad is the vibration
of the temple drums)*

*(You have thousands of eyes,
and yet You have no eyes.
You have thousands of forms,
and yet You do not have even one)*

*(You have thousands of Lotus
Feet, and yet You do not have
even one foot. You have no
nose, but you have thousands
of noses. This Play of Yours
entrances me)*
(Amongst all is the Light-You are that Light)

*(By this Illumination, that Light
is radiant within all)*

*(Through the Guru's Teachings,
the Light shines forth)*

*(That which is pleasing to Him
is the lamp-lit worship service)*

*(My mind is enticed by the honey-
sweet Lotus Feet of the Lord. Day
and night, I thirst for them)*

*(Bestow the Water of Your Mercy
upon Nanak, the thirsty song-bird,
so that he may come to dwell in Your Name)*

Dhan Guru Nanak Dev ji

Guru Nanak taught the congregation at Jagannath Puri how nature's tributes to the Creator was superior to any ritualistic oblation offered before images. Hypocrisy and rituals are of no avail and no match to simplicity and sincere prayer. Similarly, there are a number of *sabdas* (hymns) in the Guru Granth Sahib by *bhagats* that preach the same thing. **Ravidas**'s hymn begins with the line, "Lord, Thy name to me is the *arti* and holy ablutions. All else is a false show." (SGGS, 694). Says **Sen**, "May I be a sacrifice unto the Lord: that for me is the *arti* performed with lamps, *ghee* and incense" (SGGS, 695). **Kabir**'s hymn is in the same vein. It says, "Brothers! That is how the Immaculate Lord's *arti* is made ……Let divine essence be the oil, the Lords Name the wick, and enlightened self the lamp. Lighting this lamp we invoke the Lord"

(SGGS, 1350). **Dhanna**'s hymn is simply a prayer for the common needs of life (SGGS, 695).

The sky is the salver

And the sun and moon the lamps.

The luminous stars in the heavens are
the pearls.

Scented air from the sandal-clad hills is
the incense,

The winds make the fan for Thee,

And the vast forests wreaths of flowers.

The un-struck music of creation is the
trumpet.

Thus goes on the *arti* (adoration) for
Thee,

O Thou dispeller of doubt and fear!

\-   **Guru Nanak**

BIBLIOGRAPHY

1. The Encyclopedia of Sikhism (IV Volumes) – Harbans Singh (Editor-in Chief)

2. The Sikh Religion (Six Volumes) – M. A. Macauliffe

3. A History of the Sikhs (Two Volumes) – Khushwant Singh

4. The Sikhs Today – Khushwant Singh

5. Evolution of the Khalsa (Two Volumes) – Indubhusan Banerjee

6. The Sikhs and their Scriptures – C. H. Loehlin

7. A Brief Account of the Sikh People - Ganda Singh

8. Glimpses of the Sikh Gurus – Mukhtar Singh Goraya

9. The Sikhs - W. Owen Cole and Piara Singh Sambhi

10. The Great Divide – H. V. Hodson

11. The Sikh People Yesterday and Today – K. S. Duggal

12. Robber noblemen – Joyce Pettigrew

13. History of India (1000-1707A.D.) – A. L. Srivastava

14. History of India – D. N. and S. D. Kundra

15. Internet (Wikipedia, the free encyclopedia)